Black Violet TAROT

Heidi Phelps

ROCKPOOL

ACKNOWLEDGMENTS

It takes a village to learn tarot, and an even bigger village to design a tarot deck, put it out into the world, and spread the word about it. Much love and thanks go to the following people who have helped, inspired, and supported me along the way: Erdem and Leyla Dedebas, Andrea Phelps, Lisa Phelps, Amanda Sadler, Natalie Levy-Costa, Mercedes Ortiz-Olivieri, Shannon Sheridan, Melissa Cynova, and Lily Howell.

A Rockpool book
PO Box 252
Summer Hill NSW 2130
Australia

rockpoolpublishing.com

Follow us! **f** 📷 rockpoolpublishing
Tag your images with #rockpoolpublishing

Originally self-published by Heidi Phelps as *The Black Violet Tarot*, 2021

This edition published in 2024 by Rockpool Publishing

ISBN: 9781922786227

Copyright text and illustrations © Heidi Phelps 2024
Copyright design © Rockpool Publishing 2024

Edited by Lisa Macken
Design and typesetting by Sara Lindberg,
Rockpool Publishing

All rights reserved. No part of this publication may be reproduced, stored in a retrieval system, or transmitted in any form or by any means, electronic, mechanical, photocopying, recording or otherwise, without the prior written permission of the publisher.

Printed and bound in China
10 9 8 7 6 5 4 3 2 1

CONTENTS

Introduction ♦ 2

How to use the cards ♦ 4

Card spreads ♦ 7

Major arcana: life lessons ♦ 11

Minor arcana: everyday life events ♦ 61

Swords ♦ 62

Pentacles ♦ 90

Wands ♦ 118

Cups ♦ 146

About the author ♦ 174

INTRODUCTION

Throughout history, art, and folklore, violets have represented life and fertility, death, and remembrance: a striking contrast of joy versus grief, beginning versus end, and future versus memory. Designed entirely in black and white, the illustrations in this deck reflect this idea of bittersweet dualities: of shining a light in times of darkness.

Black Violet Tarot was a labor of love I created while my mother was dying from cancer, and while I was pregnant with my daughter, Leyla. It was simultaneously the happiest and saddest time in my life, as I navigated the two extremes of joy and grief at once. One didn't cancel out or dull the other. I started learning tarot when my mom was first diagnosed with cancer, and while I was undergoing fertility treatments to conceive my first child. At the time tarot was a form of escapism, of getting lost in the stories of the fool's journey in the major arcana; the gains and losses throughout the suit of Pentacles; of intellect, determination, and even deception in the suit of Swords; the emotional rollercoaster of the Cups; and the creative energy and manifestation of the Wands.

Learning the stories of tarot, of the overall structure, the suits, and then the intricate stories contained within each individual card seemed overwhelming at first. I decided to break it down one card at a time, studying its meaning and symbolism, and eventually taking its key themes and designing my own interpretation of it. I didn't initially set out to create a deck, but the more I learned and drew the more I wanted to keep going – and so the path to creating this tarot deck began.

As my mother's illness worsened, and after I became pregnant with Leyla after my first round of in vitro fertilization, this creative exercise seemed even more critical for staying grounded. Facing the enormity of losing my mom, and becoming a parent for the first time, would've felt impossible if I looked at it all as a whole. I started to see that illustrating the tarot one card at a time helped me process all the emotions I was feeling one day at a time.

There were no rules for how I approached this project, no tarot police saying I had to execute this deck in any specific way. I had the comforting structure of a cartomancy system, with the flexibility to choose the card I wanted to work on each day: engaging with what felt right in that moment, skipping what didn't. That's how I was able to navigate through my grief, and celebrate my joy.

An interesting thing happened as I started sharing my story and creative process. People started reaching out to share their own stories of joy and grief and their stories of how tarot helped them get through it. Other artists, writers and artisans started using the deck to tell their own stories through their respective mediums. Writers used this tarot to spark inspiration for short stories, and a vegan candle company developed scent profiles for candles, inspired by my Empress, Hierophant, Judgment, and High Priestess cards. A floral designer created arrangements inspired by the Death, High Priestess, and The Lovers cards.

Sharing my work and story helped me see what a powerful tool tarot is for processing and healing whatever emotions you're working through, and for sparking new ideas and creativity. In that spirit, *Black Violet Tarot* is a deck is for anyone who wants to reflect on any aspect of life – joyful or painful, meaningful or mundane – to tap into their creativity and artistic voice.

HOW TO USE THE CARDS

The *Black Violet Tarot* deck is meant to spark inspiration for art and self-expression. Use it as a tool to reflect on what is and dream about what could be, whether you're putting pen to paper, fingers to keyboard, stylus to screen, brush to canvas, or ingredients to cutting board.

In this booklet you'll find possible meanings for each card in the deck, inspired by and sometimes diverging from the Rider-Waite-Smith tarot archetypes. These descriptions are not prescriptions for the exact meaning or lesson you must extract from each card, but are merely starting points. My hope is that when you pull the cards, either individually or in a spread, you'll use your intuition to derive your own interpretation that feels relevant to you. This booklet can help jog some ideas if you're stuck.

For each reading I recommend taking a moment to meditate on what feelings, visions, memories, or concepts come to you when you encounter a card or combination of cards. Let's say you pull The Empress card, number III in the major arcana, who represents a major life lesson. Looking at the illustration, you'll see The Empress with 12 stars scattered throughout her hair, and she is carrying a bouquet and is surrounded by trees, butterflies, and flowers. What about this image resonates with you? Are you drawn mostly to the flowers, her hands, the leaves in the trees . . . or something else? What does this card make you think of?

Pause to recognize where this train of thought leads you. Maybe you start to remember a time you went hiking in the woods with your best friend and briefly lost your way. What lessons did you learn that day, if any? Start recording, sketching out, sculpting, or using collage – whatever medium you like – the emotions you felt while it was happening. Were you scared or nervous? What did you see, smell, hear, taste, or touch? Are there characters, real or imaginary, that would be interesting to add into this scene? Could this be the start of a short story or comic strip? Maybe, or maybe not, but even just letting your memories and imagination take over – preferably unedited, to start – is an important part of any creative process.

In building this women-led tarot deck I struggled at first with what to do with the traditionally masculine cards of the original Rider-Waite-Smith tarot. I thought of renaming them or creating new characters entirely, but then I realized I was overthinking it and that the answer was ridiculously simple. Every human embodies both masculine and feminine qualities and characteristics, and all people whether male, female, or gender fluid or non-binary are capable of authority and power, and worthy of respect. These cards are archetypes that inspire us to look within ourselves and explore what we're capable of.

Pips and court cards

Pips are the aces through to ten of each suit. Ace cards represent the overall vibe of the suit and the themes you can expect to see in the subsequent cards, and each number after the ace has common themes across suits; for example, twos represent balance and decision-making, while fives suggest conflict. Creating lists of common themes in numbers across suits could be a potentially helpful creative exercise for establishing connections between different scenarios and concepts.

With the four suits:

- Swords represent change, transformation, and intellect, and the suit is associated with the element of air.
- Pentacles represent security, finances, and growth, and the suit is associated with the element of earth.
- Wands represent inspiration, creativity, and ambition, and the suit is associated with the element of fire.
- Cups represent emotions, relationships, and personal connections, and the suit is associated with the element of water.

Court cards usually represent a person, either you or someone in your life, and there is a particular personality type associated with each court card. When they appear in a reading, think about who they might remind you of: yourself, a family member, colleague, friend, romantic partner, or neighbor. Derive meaning based on the surrounding cards, where they appear in the spread, and, most importantly, what your intuition brings up when confronted with the card.

Have fun, and see where your tarot cards take you. Consider sharing your art and asking for additional ideas or feedback on social media with hashtag #BlackVioletTarot. Together we can grow our community of artists and dreamers.

CARD SPREADS

There are so many spreads to choose from when you're starting to learn tarot, or even for seasoned readers. I could include the ubiquitous Celtic Cross or a typical three-card past/present/future spread, which I love and use all the time, but I thought it would be more useful to craft some of my own. The spreads outlined below are not necessarily conventional, but I hope they can provide some insight. They are designed to help you navigate through daily life, spark creative inspiration, and work through creative projects. As always, take what you like and leave the rest.

Daily inspiration

This spread will spark everyday creative magic. Feel free to modify it to suit your preferences: you can add more cards for clarification, additional depth, or to dig deeper into specific aspects of your creative possibilities.

- Card 1, theme of the day: This card represents the overall energy or theme to consider focusing on for the day. It can set the tone for your creative work, and/or get your mind on a train of thought that can start generating new ideas.
- Card 2, creative block: This card addresses potential obstacles you may encounter today that could derail your creative flow. Now's a good time to go through what you can do to overcome these obstacles should they occur.
- Card 3, creative spark: This card signifies creative opportunities available to you today, and offers guidance on where to look for inspiration, how to get and stay motivated, and how to tap into your creative potential.

Weekly navigation

This spread will help you get through the coming week in one piece.

- Card 1, theme of the week: What overarching theme or idea should you focus on this week?
- Card 2, challenge to overcome: What obstacles or challenges may come up this week?
- Card 3, action to take: How can you handle those obstacles or challenges?
- Card 4, advice from within: What inner wisdom can you tap into to guide you through your week?
- Card 5, external influence: What external factors might impact your week, positively or negatively?
- Card 6, focus and priorities: Where is the best place to direct your time and energy?
- Card 7, outcome or lesson: What lesson did you learn that you can take with you into next week?

Project kick-off

This spread is for when you begin your next big creative endeavor.

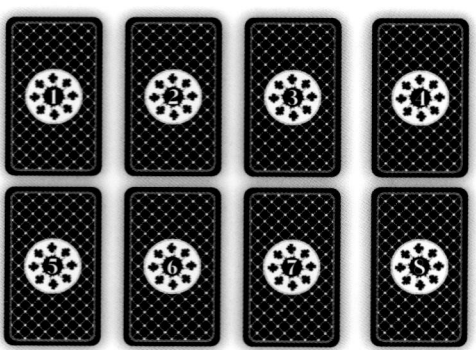

- Card 1, vision: Use this card to clarify and solidify your goal for the project.
- Card 2, challenges: Potential challenges or setbacks that may pop up along the way.
- Card 3, guidance: Guidance for navigating these challenges, or approaching the project.
- Card 4, creative energy: A potential source that might boost your creative flow.
- Card 5, inspiration: Places you can turn to when you need inspiration along the way.
- Card 6, collaboration: People to partner with or consult to amplify the impact of your project.
- Card 7, outcome: The best place to direct your time, resources, and energy.
- Card 8, final advice: Additional advice to keep in mind as you embark on this new project.

MAJOR ARCANA

LIFE LESSONS

The major arcana incorporate the first 22 cards in the deck and tell the story of a life's journey, starting from card 0, The Fool, who sets off to explore the unknown. While traveling through the major arcana The Fool encounters a series of archetypes that teach her important life lessons, lessons that we too can learn from. Her journey concludes with card 21, The World, a card that signifies completion and accomplishment.

Two bonus cards have been included with the major arcana: Ghost, and Coven. I created them during the Halloween season of 2022. Inspired by the holiday, I took two concepts that are meant to "scare" us – ghosts and witches – and, instead, used them to offer the reader a sense of solidarity and self-compassion. Coven celebrates the support you receive from your closest friends and confidantes, and Ghost encourages you to embrace your humanity (imperfections and all) and forgive yourself for past mistakes. Essentially, these two bonus cards encourage you to re-examine your relationship with fear, and fully acknowledge your tenacity and resilience.

0. THE FOOL

♦

TRUST, HOPE, INFINITE POTENTIAL

The Fool is card 0 in the deck, a number of infinite potential and fresh beginnings. She sets out on a new path, hopeful and unafraid of what's to come – partly because she's brave, and partly because she doesn't have enough experience yet to know what potential challenges lie ahead of her. This card embodies an endearing innocence and naiveté as she looks up to the sky, full of hopes and daydreams, blissfully unaware (or maybe uninterested?) in the fact that she's standing on the edge of a cliff, about to plunge into unknown territory. The Fool indicates you're on the brink of starting a different journey in your life such as a project, move, or new job or relationship, and encourages you to move forward to see where it will take you.

REVERSED
IRRESPONSIBILITY, RECKLESSNESS, GULLIBILITY

The Fool reversed suggests you may be proceeding too recklessly into unknown territory. Somebody may be misleading you into a false sense of security, or you may be throwing caution to the wind. Either way, you need to slow down and plan your next steps more carefully. Very often when people pull a reversed card I like to encourage them to reflect on what the card looks like upside down. Upright, The Fool looks like she's going to confidently leap into the unknown. Reversed, it almost looks as though the cliff is holding her back: as though she has fallen upside down and is powerless and suspended. This suggests that you may not be ready to take this leap right now. Maybe there are things you need to learn or do first, or maybe you're being held back for reasons beyond your control. Either way, it's okay: you'll know when the time is right.

I. THE MAGICIAN

◆

VISION, POWER, MANIFESTATION

At the end of *The Wizard of Oz* the lion finds out he always had courage, the scarecrow already had a brain, the tin man had a heart, and Dorothy always had the power to return home. That's the spirit of The Magician: suggesting that you have everything you need to make your dreams come to fruition. You have the drive, power, skills, and energy to manifest whatever new project or idea you envision. It won't necessarily come easily, though, and you'll still need to lay out a plan, strategize, and do the work – but you're more than capable of making it happen.

REVERSED

TRICKERY, MANIPULATION, UNTAPPED POTENTIAL

When this card is held upside down, all the elements The Magician needs to put on her magic show seem to fall away from her. The birds fly away from her body, flames fall out of her hands and extinguish themselves, and the flowers are uprooted from the ground. This suggests these tools were merely artifice, that they were used to manipulate and trick The Magician's audience into thinking, doing, or believing what she wants them to. Maybe she's a fraudster at heart, or maybe she's relying on deception instead of doing the work to make true magic and put actual good into the world but, either way, this card reversed warns you of someone who may be giving you false illusions. Alternatively, perhaps it's you that's not representing yourself authentically to others, or even to yourself. Take a moment to reflect on who you're surrounding yourself with, whose advice you're following, or how you're representing yourself to others. Your current situation may call for more honesty and transparency.

II. THE HIGH PRIESTESS

◆

INTUITION, EMPATHY, MYSTERY

A partner to the Hierophant (card V), The High Priestess is a teacher and guide who can help you unlock life's mysteries. Navigating gracefully between the conscious and subconscious realms, The High Priestess invites you to remain still: to pause, reflect, and listen to your intuition as you determine your next steps. Things may feel confusing or unclear right now and there are likely some hidden forces at play, so The High Priestess urges you to trust your instincts as you move forward. Your path will become clearer as you go.

REVERSED
CONFUSION, INDECISIVENESS, HESITATION

You've got a lot of questions right now, and don't trust yourself to know the right answers. This can be a scary feeling, but it doesn't have to be. We've all had times where we've second-guessed ourselves or felt lost, so know that you're not alone in feeling this way. This often happens when, deep inside, you know what you want but your desires, needs, and gut instincts get drowned out by outside voices.

This could be a great time to turn inward and take a good, honest look at the situation: what you want, what you need, and what feels right for you. Trust that you know enough and have seen enough to determine your own path without having to rely on other people's opinions or ideas. Similarly, beware of people giving out bad advice, even if it's well intended. What has worked for some people won't necessarily work for you, and it may be time to carve out your own path.

III. THE EMPRESS

◆

FERTILITY, CREATIVITY, SENSUALITY

The Empress is the Mother Earth figure of the tarot deck and represents fertility. She often heralds a birth or pregnancy, but can also represent the birth of a fresh idea, project, or creative period in your life. When you encounter The Empress, know that you're walking on fertile ground where new life is about to grow. She encourages you to embrace, cultivate, and nurture it, and fully experience it with all your senses. The Empress can also pop up when you need to experience pure pleasure. It's easy to get so caught up in your daily tasks and what you have to do that you forget to incorporate the things you love to do, the things that make you feel happy and whole. Whether it's taking a walk in the woods, getting your hands dirty in your garden, lighting that fancy candle you've been saving, or making yourself your very favorite dish, take some time out to treat your senses.

REVERSED
NEGLECT, DETACHMENT, LACK OF INSPIRATION

The Empress card reversed can suggest a lack of nurturing, abundance, or creativity. You may feel detached from your creative energy and intuition, or have difficulty expressing yourself effectively. As a result, you may have difficulty bringing your ideas to fruition (or thinking of new ideas, to begin with). You may also have trouble caring for yourself and others, which can have a negative impact on your most important relationships. While the upright Empress signifies fertility and growth, the reversed position could signify a need to address stagnant or blocked energy. This card encourages self-care, reflection, and a re-evaluation of how you nurture yourself and your aspirations.

> ### AUTHOR'S NOTE
>
> As both a visual artist and mom whose journey toward motherhood came joyfully but not easily, The Empress is a card that's close to my heart.

IV. THE EMPEROR

◆

POWER, AUTHORITY, INFRASTRUCTURE

The Emperor stands on a hill overlooking her kingdom. She holds a staff with a ram's head on it, symbolizing Aries and the planet Mars and a strong, warrior spirit. The Emperor is considered to be the father figure of the tarot deck, and suggests you may be taking on a fatherly role – regardless of whether you're male, female, or non-binary. Alternatively, a paternal figure in your life may be particularly important to you at this time. Now might be an opportune time to step into your power and lay the groundwork for projects you have wanted to take on, by yourself or with the guidance of someone you respect and trust.

REVERSED
OPPRESSION, MISTREATMENT, ABUSE OF POWER

The Emperor reversed suggests challenges in asserting leadership or maintaining order, which could mean a couple of things. You may be having trouble asserting authority or establishing yourself as a leader in your line of work, family, or community. If this is the case, know that when you second-guess your own abilities other people will also second-guess them: you can't expect others to have more faith in you than you have in yourself. On the other hand, this card reversed could represent an abuse of power, that you are exerting excessive control over others and not taking other people's perspectives into consideration. Instead of wielding authority, it's important to seek balance, collaboration, and adaptability. A reversed Emperor prompts introspection into your own authority dynamics and the importance of finding a more flexible and inclusive approach to leadership.

AUTHOR'S NOTE

As a kid of a single mom, I can personally attest to one person's ability to embody both the authority and protection of The Emperor along with the creativity, love, and compassion of The Empress (card III).

V. THE HIEROPHANT

◆

WISDOM, GUIDANCE, CURIOSITY

The Hierophant represents the balance between the conscious and subconscious minds. She's a teacher and guide who unlocks mysteries and deciphers codes, suggesting that you may be learning something new and could benefit from sage knowledge and advice. She also represents tradition and conventionality, having built her own tried-and-true methods for understanding the world through centuries of dedicated work and experimentation. The Hierophant suggests you may benefit from taking better-known approaches to learning, problem solving, and decision-making. It may seem as though you're playing it safe, but it could just be what the situation calls for right now.

REVERSED

MISDIRECTION, LACK OF SELF-CONFIDENCE, POOR COUNSEL

The Hierophant reversed signifies a departure from traditional beliefs, institutions, and tried-and-true methods. It suggests a period of questioning established norms and seeking your own path. Now may not be the time to play it safe; instead, you might benefit from experimentation and leaning toward an unorthodox, nonconformist way of thinking. Similar to the advice given when the High Priestess (card II) is reversed, a reversed Hierophant cautions you against people who give out bad advice, even if it's well intended. Now is not the time to seek guidance from people with rigid, conformist ideas and perspectives, as they may not lead you in the direction you need to go – mainly because they've never been able to get there themselves.

AUTHOR'S NOTE

The Rider-Waite-Smith version of The Hierophant makes references to the pope and is the male counterpart to The High Priestess. The *Black Violet Tarot* nods to these ideas by incorporating traditional masculine/papal signifiers; for example, the shape of her hair resembles a pope's hat. This deck's Hierophant works in tandem with The High Priestess.

VI. THE LOVERS

◆

LOVE, HARMONY, SYMBIOSIS

Consider The Lovers card a shoutout to the most loving and meaningful relationships in your life, showing gratitude for the ones who lift you up and push you to be a better person. This could refer to romantic relationships, friendships, family relationships with biological or chosen family members, or even a particularly productive and supportive business partnership. Love doesn't have one unique definition; it comes in many forms. Revel in the beauty of whatever form love takes for you.

REVERSED

DISCONNECTION, ISOLATION, MISCOMMUNICATION

The Lovers reversed suggests disharmony in relationships and decisions driven by conflict or confusion. It can also indicate walls you've built up to emotionally protect yourself that are preventing people from connecting with you on a non-superficial level. This reversal could indicate past trauma related to personal intimacy, or a lack of alignment between heart and mind. It can serve as a well-intended but non-judgmental nudge to let your guard down a little, to allow more communication, love, and trust into your life. Alternatively, it might signify the need for self-love and reflection before entering a partnership. Whatever the case may be, a reversed Lovers card prompts you to assess your values and priorities, and potentially address any unresolved issues before entering into a relationship. By seeking clarity and open dialogue, you can navigate the complexities and restore balance to matters of the heart.

VII. THE CHARIOT

◆

CONFIDENCE, DETERMINATION, PERSEVERANCE

See how she charges forward on her chariot, confidently controlling the horses – and without actually holding onto any reins. That sums up The Chariot perfectly: charging forward with confidence and conviction, controlling situations solely with her willpower and determination. Simply put, The Chariot encourages you to keep going no matter what obstacles appear in your path, or how difficult the road ahead may be.

REVERSED
POWERLESSNESS, DEFEAT, OBSESSION

The Chariot reversed signifies a loss of control, direction, or inner drive, which suggests obstacles or internal conflicts that hinder progress and momentum. Decisions may be impulsive or lack a clear strategy. This reversal could reflect a sense of being pulled in different directions, causing frustration and indecision. It's a reminder to regain focus, overcome inner turmoil, and re-establish your purpose. By addressing internal conflicts and clarifying goals, you can steer back onto a productive path. A reversed Chariot encourages you to find balance, harness your energy, and regain control over your ambitions and endeavors.

VIII. STRENGTH

◆

COURAGE, CONFIDENCE, COMPASSION

Strength represents the ability to control challenging situations, not with threats or violence against others but by demonstrating love, compassion, and determination. It can also suggest an ability or need to treat yourself with love and compassion, to tame your inner voice when it's too harsh or self-critical. Depicting a woman gently interacting with a lion symbolizes the ability to manage instincts and emotions with grace. Strength encourages tapping into your inner power and resilience, demonstrating control without force. It signifies a time of inner healing and the capacity to deal with life's trials with a calm and confident demeanor. Ultimately, Strength teaches that true power arises from a balanced blend of physical, emotional, and spiritual forces, highlighting the potency of gentleness and empathy in conquering both external obstacles and internal struggles.

REVERSED

WEAKNESS, FATIGUE, HARM TO SELF OR OTHERS

When reversed Strength suggests a potential lack of inner harmony and control over your emotions and impulses. This reversal could point to self-doubt, exhaustion, weakness, or a struggle to manage challenges with grace. There might be a tendency to give in to fear or let negative emotions overpower reason, sometimes out of mere fatigue. However, Strength reversed serves as a reminder to address any self-limiting beliefs and find ways to regain confidence and composure. It emphasizes the need to cultivate inner strength and patience, as well as to avoid power struggles or attempts to dominate situations through force. It's a call to work on emotional resilience and find ways to channel assertiveness constructively.

IX. THE HERMIT

◆

INTROSPECTION, REFLECTION, ALONE TIME

The Hermit card embodies introspection, solitude, and inner wisdom. Depicting a solitary woman on an island holding a single candle, and surrounding herself with candles as her only form of light, it symbolizes the search for truth and enlightenment through self-reflection. This card signifies a period of withdrawal from external distractions to seek answers from within. It suggests the value of solitude for personal growth, encouraging a deeper understanding of yourself and the world. The Hermit's candle guides her way through darkness, indicating the pursuit of knowledge and spiritual insight. It's a reminder to take time for introspection, meditation, and soul searching, leading to a renewed sense of purpose.

Now might be the time when you'll benefit from solitude, and to have your own thoughts and check in with yourself. This goes for introverts, extroverts, and anyone in between, because no matter how busy life gets it's important to carve out some downtime to reflect on how you're feeling, what's on your mind, and what you need to best take care of yourself.

REVERSED

ISOLATION, LONELINESS, DISCONNECTION

When reversed The Hermit suggests a resistance to self-reflection and a reluctance to seek inner guidance. This reversal might signify a period of avoiding solitude or ignoring the need for introspection, perhaps from a fear of facing your thoughts and emotions and leading to a sense of confusion or disconnection. It's a reminder that seeking external validation or distractions might hinder personal growth and clarity. Reversed, this card encourages a reconsideration of the benefits of introspection, solitude, and spiritual exploration. It's a call to address any avoidance tendencies and embrace the lessons that self-discovery can bring.

X. WHEEL OF FORTUNE

♦

CHANGE, PROGRESSION, CYCLES

Represented by a cycle of moon phases, Wheel of Fortune reminds you that life is continually turning, like a wheel, and represents constant change. After all, the only constant in life is change, right? Good fortune follows bad, good times shift – sometimes gradually, sometimes abruptly – to hard times and back again, and you don't have much control over what life brings your way. More often than not, you just need to roll with it. The best thing to do is to actively soak in and appreciate the beautiful, happy moments, and navigate the challenging times the best you can: asking for help when needed, and helping others when they're down.

REVERSED

FRUSTRATION, RESISTANCE TO CHANGE, RELEASE

There's a sense of incompleteness that comes with Wheel of Fortune reversed, or hitting a plateau in your journey. Something is holding you back from making progress, and it may even be you or your resistance to or fear of change. This reversal could indicate delays in achieving goals or a feeling of being stuck in a cycle. It might point to unfinished business or a need to address loose ends before moving forward, as frustrating as that may feel. This card prompts introspection into personal limitations or resistance to change. While the upright Wheel of Fortune card signifies fulfillment and accomplishment, the reversed position highlights a need to grow and adapt.

XI. JUSTICE

◆

TRUTH, FAIRNESS, ORDER

Inspired by Justitia, or Lady Justice, this card serves as a reminder that you're responsible for your actions. She's blindfolded because justice is blind, and her scale and sword help symbolize a fight for fairness, order, and balance. Notice her shadow, which was inspired by the idiom "to cast a long shadow": the idea that your actions have consequences well into the future. The Justice card embodies themes of self-evaluation, renewal, and accountability. It signifies a period of reflection on past decisions, leading to a transformational shift in consciousness, and represents the recognition of your true self and a desire for personal growth. It can spark a newfound sense of clarity as you navigate the journey ahead with a heightened sense of awareness and responsibility.

REVERSED

INJUSTICE, DISHONESTY, LACK OF FAIRNESS

When reversed Justice signifies imbalance, unfairness, or lack of accountability. It can also indicate delayed resolutions. This reversal suggests there might be a lack of equilibrium or ethical considerations in a situation. Something feels really unfair, and decisions could be clouded by bias or personal agendas. It's a reminder that fairness and truth might not prevail at the moment, and it urges you to scrutinize situations for any hidden agendas or dishonesty. A reversed Justice card prompts you to assess whether you're acting with integrity and treating others fairly, and could indicate a need to reconcile imbalances and rectify any wrongdoings. You cast a long shadow; your actions have consequences well into the future.

XII. THE HANGED ONE

◆

PAUSE, SUSPENSION, DELAY

The Hanged One reminds you that sometimes you need to pause for a while before you can move forward. This can feel frustrating when you're eager to get out of a situation, such as a job or relationship you're unhappy in, but you don't know how or aren't quite ready to make a move. There's enormous value in taking a pause to check in with yourself, figure out what you really want, and explore the options available to you.

It's worth noting that The Hanged One can untie herself from the tree at any time: there's nothing really stopping her, and she's not particularly unhappy about it. She'll be here, living in this moment, until the time is right.

REVERSED

OBSTRUCTION, OBSTACLES, SETBACKS

The Hanged One reversed can suggest a few things: a release from the obstacles that have been holding you back, or that more delays and setbacks are coming. That doesn't feel like a great answer to your questions, right? I know. Reversals can be frustrating sometimes, but the main takeaway with this card reversed is that you can be easy on yourself and let go of trying to manage factors outside your control. What you can and should do is take an honest look at the factors you can control, and channel your focus there in order to make progress. You can take charge of the situation, but not if you focus your energy in the wrong places or too much on things you have no power to change.

XIII. DEATH

♦

CHANGE, RELEASE, TRANSFORMATION

Generally speaking, Death represents change and transition, although not physical death. Don't be afraid if it shows up in a reading, because it's actually a pretty positive card. Just as the crows are released from her hair in this illustration, you're encouraged to let go of what no longer serves you in order to allow more positive influences into your life. Like death, change is inevitable and happens to everyone regardless of who you are or how strongly you try to resist it.

REVERSED
STAGNANCY, INERTIA, DENIAL

Death upright represents a period of change and transition that requires you to let go of your past, or of things in your life that no longer serve you. Death reversed suggests you're resisting making necessary changes. Maybe you're stuck in a routine that's comfortable, but not necessarily rewarding or fulfilling. Maybe you're afraid of leaving a situation you're familiar with to explore a new route that's unknown to you. What you need to remember is that sometimes, the most rewarding experiences in life are uncomfortable. They're unfamiliar, and they push you to test your boundaries in order to show you what you're capable of. Don't resist change simply because it seems scary. If heading out in a new direction has potential to help you grow and flourish, any discomfort you temporarily feel will be worth it.

AUTHOR'S NOTE

I once saw on a TV show where a character almost died from an overdose at her birthday party after pulling the Death card from her mom's tarot deck and trying to get a tattoo of it on her chest. It was a great episode but a false and unfair use of the Death card as a scary plot device/harbinger of actual death. You know better now!

XIV. TEMPERANCE

◆

BALANCE, MODERATION, CONFIDENCE

Temperance urges you to stay calm in stressful or chaotic situations. Here the woman confidently maintains her balance in the face of danger, walking on sure footing. She may even test the ropes a bit before venturing out on the wire, so she can understand what she's dealing with. Knowledge is power: you can make rational, productive decisions when you've considered all the information available.

I also like to read Temperance as a call to rest. In a society that places so much value on what we're doing and how much we're working at all times, it's worth taking a moment to check in with yourself to ask: "How am I feeling: am I burned out, or on the verge of burning out? Am I taking on too much, and do I really need to be in charge of all the tasks

I'm assigned to?" Temperance can be the signal you need to take some much-needed self-care time and do what feels truly restorative.

REVERSED

EXCESS, EXTREMES, RECKLESSNESS

I don't usually see a huge difference between the Temperance card when it's reversed versus when it's upright. In either orientation the card calls you to find balance and harmony in your life, and avoid going to extremes. It may suggest you're being impatient, impulsive, or excessive in certain areas, and could benefit from seeking out moderation and finding the equilibrium necessary for inner peace and navigating life's inevitable challenges. Depending on your situation, it can symbolize the need to take some chances. Maybe you've been playing it too safe for too long, and could benefit from bold moves. Tarot relies on your intuition to read into what the card's message can mean for you.

XV. THE DEVIL

◆

ADDICTION, SELF-SABOTAGE, BAD HABITS

The Devil urges you to confront the dark to let in the light. It's startling at first glance, but as with Death (card XIII) it can be one of the most positive cards in the deck. The Devil is all about letting go of the things – thought patterns, addictions, toxic relationships, self-sabotaging behavior, bad habits, and so on – that not only don't serve you but weigh you down and prevent you from becoming the best version of yourself. It may feel as though you're tied to these things and can't break free from them. The bad news is you are tied to them, at least for now, but the good news is you have the power to break free, whether you realize it or not. The tie is nothing but a strap that can be cut, broken, untied, or slipped out of. You just need to confront the fact that it's there, and commit to ripping it up.

REVERSED
RELEASE, FREEDOM, POSITIVE ENERGY

Think of The Devil reversed as a really good spring cleaning, where you purge the things you've been carrying around that are weighing you down and don't serve a positive purpose. It's cathartic, right? This card when reversed signifies liberation from unhealthy attachments and patterns. The reversal indicates a breaking free from addictions, obsessions, or limiting beliefs that have held you captive, and suggests a newfound awareness of your inner demons and determination to release their grip. The card highlights a pursuit of personal freedom and a refusal to be controlled by external influences. Reversed, it encourages you to confront fears and temptations, and let go of toxic connections. It prompts you to reclaim your power, make positive choices, and foster healthier relationships with yourself and others, and signifies a period of transformation where you regain control over your life and embrace a more liberated and authentic path.

XVI. THE TOWER

◆

UPHEAVAL, AWAKENING, SUDDEN CHANGE

The Tower might be an alarming card to pull, but it can be one of the most positive cards in the deck. It signals a need to burn everything to the ground in order to start anew. At times life needs to get worse before it gets better, so if you're struggling through a tough period, know that it's temporary. Live through it the best you can, because soon it'll be your time to rebuild.

The Tower card symbolizes the collapse of outdated beliefs or situations. It signifies disruption, chaos, and a breaking point that forces re-evaluation; however, its energy is transformative and clears the way for fresh beginnings. It teaches that embracing unsettling change can lead to liberation and growth. The card encourages acceptance of impermanence and the ability to find strength amid adversity, and prompts you to confront challenges with resilience.

REVERSED

AVOIDANCE, RESISTANCE, FEAR OF CHANGE

The tower is crumbling. Are you going to move forward, or are you going to cling to the rubble? This card reversed indicates change is happening, and there's not much you can do to control it. The Tower reversed represents a resistance to change and an unwillingness to step out of your comfort zone, but you'll need to find a way to heal and move on from it. It might hurt, but you'll be stronger and better off.

AUTHOR'S NOTE

This Tower illustration takes inspiration from the Maiden's Tower, or Kız Kulesi, in the Bosphorus Strait's entrance in Istanbul, Turkey. A seer predicted that the emperor's beloved daughter would be bitten by a venomous snake and die on her 18th birthday. To thwart this fate, the king ordered the construction of a tower on the islet, where he could protect her from serpents. However, on her birthday, a basket of fruit arrived with a hidden snake, causing her demise.

XVII. THE STAR

◆

HOPE, RENEWAL, HEALING

The Star comes after the crashing and burning of The Tower (card XVI) and represents starting afresh, with a renewed sense of hope and purpose. The woman is kneeling down to water the ground and add more water to a small pond, suggesting she knows she's on fertile land that's ready for new growth. This card indicates you're entering a period when everything seems possible. Persevering through past difficulties has given you a better understanding of yourself and what you're capable of: note the fact that she can see her reflection clearly in the pool of water. You have all you need to not just heal from past trauma, but to build yourself up to be stronger than you've ever been. Move forward confidently, and with appreciation for all that you have.

REVERSED

HOPELESSNESS, NEGATIVITY, SELF-DOUBT

A reversed Star suggests a temporary setback in hope and inspiration. That being said, I firmly believe The Star in either position is still a positive card. Reversed, it may just indicate that you're struggling to see all the possibility and hope that surrounds you, especially after having gone through a very challenging period. A reversed Star card invites you to address self-doubt and work through any negative thought patterns that are obstructing your sense of optimism. It prompts you to look within yourself for even the smallest spark of hope and inspiration to lead you through difficult times. Embrace self-care, meditation, and positive affirmations to help you regain your strength and hope for the future. By acknowledging your inner light and seeking support when needed, you can eventually rekindle your faith and embark on a journey of renewal and healing.

XVIII. THE MOON

◆

SUBCONSCIOUSNESS, INTUITION, FEAR

While past trauma doesn't define who you are, emotions attached to past trauma can linger in your subconscious and rise up when you least expect it, making you afraid for the future and uncertain of whom you can trust in the present. Repressed fear is represented by the crayfish, swimming just below the surface of the water. The water itself is a symbol of the subconscious mind.

There's a lot going on in this card, so here are a couple of key takeaways. The moon represents your intuition and natural instincts, which you'll need to navigate your next steps and overcome or at least manage your fears. The second thing is that tapping into your instinct and intuition is reinforced by the dog and wolf, sitting on land. One is tamed and one is wild, but they both behave in the same way instinctually: they howl at the full moon, projecting their voices throughout their territory. Your instinct and intuition are key to taking control of your current situation.

REVERSED

CATHARSIS, EPIPHANY, CLARITY

The Moon reversed signifies a period of clarity emerging from confusion and illusion. This reversal suggests that the deceptive veils that once clouded your understanding are beginning to lift. Fears and anxieties that may have been intensified in the upright position are now being recognized and confronted, enabling you to let go of them and set yourself free. A reversed Moon card encourages you to trust your intuition and instincts as they guide you through periods of uncertainty. It's a reminder to see beyond the surface, acknowledge your emotions, and embrace the truth, even if it's uncomfortable. This card prompts you to use your newfound insight to make informed decisions and navigate your path with more confidence, showing that the shadows of doubt are subsiding and allowing you to move forward with a better grasp of the situation.

XIX. THE SUN

◆

WARMTH, INNOCENCE, PURE LOVE

The Rider-Waite-Smith version of The Sun depicts a naked child riding a white horse, symbolizing strength, innocence, and vitality. It's a beautiful card, but the *Black Violet Tarot* communicates this idea with more of a maternal spin. The mother radiates warmth: so much so, the sunflowers turn toward her instead of the actual sun (the minimalist circle in the right corner). She represents the pure joy and hope that come along with the birth of a baby, and the unconditional love that bonds them forever. This card heralds a time of happiness, joy, and abundant energy: if not now, then very soon. Enjoy your time in the sun, and radiate positive energy to those around you.

REVERSED
COLDNESS, PESSIMISM, DETACHMENT

The Sun reversed signifies temporary setbacks or a delay in the full realization of joy and success. What's holding you back from making true, authentic connections with others? Alternatively, what's preventing you from looking toward the future with optimism? While the upright position symbolizes warmth, love or bonding, and positivity, a reversed Sun encourages you to examine any obstacles or self-doubts that might be hindering your connections with others, or inhibiting progress toward achieving your goals. It's a reminder to maintain a hopeful attitude despite challenges, as obstacles are often transitory. Remember that you can ask for help along the way, that vulnerability is not weakness. In fact, showing vulnerability can help you connect with people who have been through similar challenges and, at the very least, let you know you're not alone in your struggle.

A reversed Sun encourages you to address any lingering negativity or doubts, emphasizing the importance of cultivating a positive mindset. By recognizing the areas that need attention and actively working toward dispelling negativity, you can eventually allow the radiant energy of the sun to shine through once more and guide you toward success and happiness.

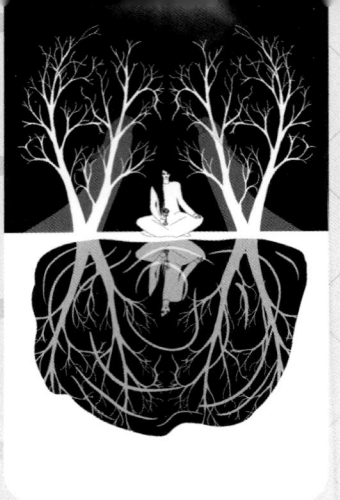

XX. JUDGMENT

◆

SELF-REFLECTION, ACCOUNTABILITY, HONESTY

The Judgment card in the Rider-Waite-Smith tarot takes inspiration from the last judgment, with women, men, and children rising from the grave to respond to Gabriel's trumpet call. My interpretation of this card is more about self-reflection and self-judgment. When you take a good look at yourself, your actions, and how you interact with others, do you like what you see? What legacy will you leave behind?

REVERSED

AVOIDANCE, WILLFUL IGNORANCE, LACK OF ACCOUNTABILITY

Judgment reversed suggests a reluctance to confront personal truths or engage in self-evaluation. This reversal could point to a fear of change, clinging to past mistakes, or resisting necessary transformations. It might indicate a struggle to break free from old patterns, leading to stagnation or missed opportunities for growth. This card encourages you to confront any self-doubt and release emotional baggage. Reversed, it can also emphasize the importance of self-forgiveness and embracing new beginnings, and prompts a reassessment of your life's direction, pushing you to let go of what no longer serves you so you can step into a phase of self-acceptance and renewal.

XXI. THE WORLD

◆

COMPLETION, ACCOMPLISHMENT, WHOLENESS

The World depicts the silhouette of a woman leaping joyfully across the night sky, throwing violets into the air against the backdrop of a full moon. The moon represents wholeness, or the completion of a moon cycle, and indicates a time when you have finished or are about to finish a major project or formative era in your life. You've accomplished a lot, and now it's time to celebrate before jumping to the next chapter.

The World in tarot is a symbol of completion, harmony, and wholeness. It marks a time of fulfillment and the attainment of goals, often indicating a period of personal growth and enlightenment, and highlights the sense that you've come full circle and reached a point of mastery. The card encourages you to celebrate your achievements while acknowledging the interconnectedness of all experiences. It's a reminder that endings are also new beginnings, and by embracing the lessons of your journey you can continue to evolve and expand your understanding of the world around you.

REVERSED
INCOMPLETION, DISCONTINUITY, LACK OF CLOSURE

The World reversed signifies a temporary delay or incomplete closure in a cycle of accomplishment. This reversal suggests there might be unfinished business or lingering loose ends preventing the full realization of your goals. While an upright World card symbolizes fulfillment and completion, the reversed position could indicate a need for further introspection and personal growth before you can fully move forward. It's a reminder to address any remaining obstacles, fears, or uncertainties that are holding you back, and prompts you to reflect on your journey and consider the lessons you've learned. It's an opportunity to tie up loose ends, seek resolution, and make necessary adjustments to ensure that you're fully prepared for the next phase. By addressing the incomplete aspects of your life, you can set the stage for a more balanced and successful future.

BONUS CARD

GHOST

◆

HAUNTING, REGRET, SELF-COMPASSION

The Ghost card features a woman who is confronted by a ghost, who holds out a small bouquet of flowers as a gift or peace offering. Neither one seems shocked to see the other, but the woman seems afraid of the ghost and what she represents. Ghost represents a confrontation between past and present, a healing from past trauma, regrets for things you did or didn't do, or fear that your past will be uncovered or will inevitably determine your future. This card empowers you to make peace with your history, because there's no need to hide or be ashamed of it. Understanding where you came from can be a powerful step in determining where you want to go, who you want to be, and what mistakes you can learn from.

> ### AUTHOR'S NOTE
>
> The gowns on each figure are blowing in two different directions, suggesting they're meant to move separate ways – which, inevitably, they will. For now they're looking each other in the eye, confronting each other, even if it feels uncomfortable. They're doing the work to understand each other before they move on.

REVERSED

AVOIDANCE, DREAD, LACK OF SELF-AWARENESS

In a reversed Ghost card the woman and ghost stand frozen by avoidance. Their faces are averted, reflecting the dread that lingers in the air. The ghost's tender offering of flowers meets unspoken rejection, symbolizing the avoidance of confronting inner fears and unresolved history. Their separate gowns billow away, mirroring a refusal to engage and heal.

This card embodies the inertia of dread and lack of self-awareness. It cautions against sidestepping the ghosts of the past, which, when ignored, grow stronger. Avoidance perpetuates a cycle of unease and restricts personal growth. The chance to understand the lessons of history is missed. Just as the gowns pull apart, so does the path to self-improvement fade when avoidance prevails. A reversed Ghost urges a breaking free from the grip of dread, and embracing self-awareness to move forward unburdened.

BONUS CARD

COVEN

◆

SISTERHOOD, SOLIDARITY, SECRETS

The keywords above may sound familiar, because Coven is meant to be a counterpart to the Three of Cups: a card of sisterhood, solidarity, and friendship. While the Three of Cups celebrates these ideas in a light, airy way, Coven represents close friendships as a form of protection. It gives a shoutout to the people in your life who have seen you at your worst and accept you as you are, without judgment. They know your secrets, and you know theirs; you will always have each other's backs. If one person in the coven needs help plotting their next steps, the rest of the group will brainstorm, think things through, or call you on your bullsh*t.

REVERSED
JEALOUSY, BITTERNESS, TOXIC BONDS

In Coven reversed, the once unbreakable circle of sisterhood becomes tainted with jealousy and bitterness. The sense of protection and acceptance that once united friends now unravels into unhealthy dynamics. Secrets turn to weapons, and the bond meant to uplift morphs into a toxic quagmire.

This card delves into the darker side of friendship, highlighting the potential for jealousy and resentment to fester. The very people who once supported each other now harbor negativity, eroding the foundation of trust. The collective brainstorming and solidarity have given way to competitive thoughts and divisive intentions. As the coven fractures it reveals the dangers of unhealthy relationships. A reversed Coven stands as a cautionary tale, reminding you that friendships can turn sour when not nurtured with genuine care and respect. It underscores the need to address issues openly and honestly before they irreparably poison the bonds you hold dear.

While an upright Coven celebrates unity, a reversed Coven serves as a reminder to recognize and rectify the presence of jealousy and bitterness within friendships. It calls for introspection, communication, and the courage to release toxic connections for the sake of emotional well-being.

MINOR ARCANA

EVERYDAY LIFE EVENTS

ACE of SWORDS

◆

SKILL, STRENGTH, EMPOWERMENT

The Ace of Swords ushers in a whole new burst of intellectual energy that empowers you to move forward with confidence and skill, equipped to take on any challenge that comes your way. The path ahead may be challenging – some of the more formative periods in our lives often are – but you're capable of overcoming any obstacle once you set your mind to it. The woman's confident grip on her sword signifies her mastery of her own capabilities and her ability to wield her intellect effectively. In that spirit, the Ace of Swords invites you to tap into your inner strength and skill set to overcome challenges. It's an invitation to feel empowered to cut through confusion to gain a sharp understanding of situations and find innovative solutions.

REVERSED

CONFUSION, UNPREPAREDNESS, CLOUDED JUDGMENT

The Ace of Swords reversed suggests that the surge of mental clarity and breakthrough typically represented by the Ace of Swords is hindered. It cautions against making hasty decisions and overestimating your capabilities, and signifies a need to untangle your thoughts before taking action as clouded judgment might lead to decisions you'll come to regret later. This card prompts you to approach situations with caution and ensure you have all the necessary information before proceeding. By acknowledging the potential for confusion and unpreparedness, you can navigate challenges with greater wisdom. A reversed Ace of Swords is a reminder to take the time to clarify your thoughts and gain a clear perspective before making decisions, enabling you to overcome obstacles via a more measured and thoughtful approach.

TWO of SWORDS

♦

OPTIONS, LOGIC, EMOTION

The Two of Swords represents selecting between two options. It may be difficult to choose a clear path right now because both options may seem equally good or equally bad. Though swords typically represent intellect you'll notice she's surrounded by water, which symbolizes emotions. This card suggests you need to tap into logic and emotion to make the decision that's best for you. The card portrays a moment of decision-making where she must balance her rationality and feelings. It calls for a balanced approach that takes both sides into account, reflecting the inner conflict that comes with important choices. By acknowledging the duality of your thoughts and feelings you can make decisions that resonate deeply and make use of your intellect. The Two of Swords encourages you to make choices that align with your true desires and highest sense of self.

REVERSED

INDECISION, BEING OVERWHELMED, HESITATION

A reversed Two of Swords suggests a state of inner conflict and uncertainty, where the woman's crossed swords – now depicted upside down – reflect her difficulty with making a clear choice. This reversal prompts you to acknowledge the feeling of being overwhelmed caused by conflicting options. Your hesitation may stem from analysis paralysis, or an inability to choose a path forward from fear of making the wrong decision or not having all the information you need.

This card serves as a reminder to address your indecision and seek ways to overcome it. It encourages you to take a step back, gain perspective, and explore your options more thoroughly. By confronting your uncertainties and finding strategies to manage overwhelming choices, you can navigate challenges with greater clarity and confidence. A reversed Two of Swords invites you to embrace the power of choice, even if it requires overcoming your initial hesitation.

THREE of SWORDS

♦

SADNESS, HEARTBREAK, LIFE LESSONS

This card symbolizes the pain of emotional wounds caused by heartache, disappointment, or betrayal; however, it also carries the potential for profound life lessons. It suggests you're going through a rough period marked by pain, heartbreak, and sadness but, like the clouds raining on the heart and sword, it's temporary. Better days are on the horizon, so you just need to get through this rough patch the best you can.

The Three of Swords prompts you to embrace the transformative power of pain. Your trials can lead to greater emotional understanding, empathy for others, and resilience to overcome future obstacles. The card serves as a reminder to acknowledge your feelings of sadness and hurt while also recognizing the opportunities for growth and self-discovery they offer. It encourages you to find the silver lining and seek wisdom in the midst of heartache. By navigating through life's challenges with an open heart and a willingness to learn, you can turn the Three of Swords into a stepping stone toward deeper emotional insight and healing.

REVERSED

HOPE, RELEASE, FORGIVENESS

When the Three of Swords is flipped upside down you can imagine the swords breaking free from the heart, falling to the ground and allowing the heart to begin to heal. With the heart no longer pierced by swords, this card reversed indicates a gradual healing process from heartbreak and a time when you're beginning to find solace and relief.

A reversed Three of Swords prompts you to embrace the hope that comes after a period of suffering, and signifies a willingness to release negative emotions and let go of past hurts. Whenever I pull this card in reverse I think about how holding on to anger is like drinking poison, and that forgiveness of those who have hurt you or of yourself is an essential step toward emotional freedom. This card serves as a reminder to focus on healing and self-care, because by releasing the weight of past pain and fostering forgiveness you can create space for hope to flourish.

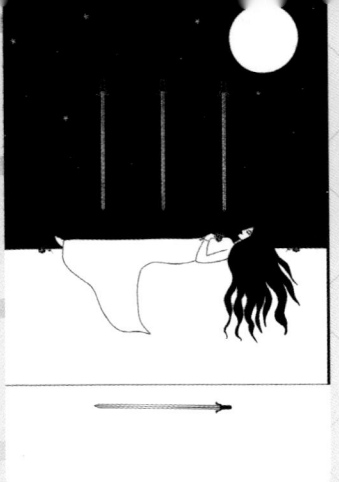

FOUR of SWORDS

♦

REST, RECUPERATION, RECHARGING

The Four of Swords deals with the aftermath of the struggle in the Three of Swords, because that was a tough situation and it's time to rest and recuperate. This is the #selfcare card: you need to pause and recover from the hardships you've endured before moving forward. It's possible you have more challenges in the near future, and you're going to need to recharge to regain enough energy and mental clarity to tackle them. Things might be hard, but you can endure hard things.

> **AUTHOR'S NOTE**
>
> Things that usually help me when I'm in a funk include sleep, leisurely walks, low-key hangouts with friends, petting kitties, visiting dog parks, making silly faces at kids in strollers, turning off the news, and paying attention to simply breathing.

REVERSED

FATIGUE, DEJECTION, APATHY

A reversed Four of Swords embodies themes of lingering fatigue, prolonged dejection, and persistent apathy. This card suggests that despite attempts to rest and recuperate you may still find it challenging to overcome exhaustion and emotional weariness. The woman's position remains restless, reflecting an ongoing struggle to find solace. When reversed this card prompts you to address the underlying causes of your fatigue and dejection, and signifies a need to delve deeper into the sources of your emotional exhaustion and seek the appropriate support to overcome it.

This card serves as a reminder to be proactive in seeking healing and self-care. It encourages you to confront any apathy that might be holding you back and engage in activities that revitalize your spirit. By acknowledging your emotions and seeking ways to reignite your enthusiasm you can gradually move beyond the cycle of fatigue and dejection, and find renewed motivation to navigate life's challenges with greater resilience.

FIVE of SWORDS

◆

CONFLICT, BATTLE, FUTILITY

The Five of Swords depicts a falling out or argument in which nobody is truly the winner. One woman walks away in defeat, exhausted, sad, and dropping her sword. The other woman may have technically won this battle, but it's an empty victory as both women are tired, depleted, and distrustful of one another. The ends don't justify the means. This card is a reminder to keep your ego in check and choose your battles wisely. You don't have to get your way all the time, and you don't need to steamroll over others to get what you want.

REVERSED
RESOLUTION, COMPROMISE, COMPASSION

A reversed Five of Swords suggests a turning point where conflicts are being resolved and tensions easing. The women in the card may be starting to shift away from confrontation toward understanding. When reversed this card prompts you to consider finding common ground and seeking solutions that promote harmony. It signifies a willingness to let go of ego-driven battles and embrace a more compassionate approach to interactions.

An upside-down Five of Swords serves as a reminder to practice empathy and view situations from different perspectives, and encourages you to engage in open dialogue and seek compromises that benefit all of the parties involved. By prioritizing resolution over winning, you can foster healthier relationships and create an atmosphere of cooperation. It invites you to rise above petty conflicts, showing kindness and understanding in your interactions and ultimately leading to more positive outcomes and connections.

SIX of SWORDS

◆

HOPE, OPTIMISM, OVERCOMING HARDSHIP

The Six of Swords is a card of hope. You've gone through a very difficult period – note the scribbly, choppy waters – but you're on your way to something better for you and your loved ones. This card is all of us at some point, getting through challenging times the best we can and setting our sights on a better future. Together, we always get there.

> ### AUTHOR'S NOTE
>
> This card was created in the middle of the COVID-19 pandemic, at the tail end of four long years of the Trump administration. When Trump officially lost the election it definitely felt like the United States, as a country, community, and collective, was on its way to better times.

REVERSED
DEFEAT, RETREAT, ACCEPTANCE OF THE STATUS QUO

A reversed Six of Swords in tarot embodies themes of defeat, stalled progress, and a reluctant acceptance of the status quo. This card suggests that despite a desire to move forward there may be obstacles preventing you from making the desired changes. The boat, when reversed, seems to reflect a stillness that nods to a sense of being stuck or unable to escape challenging circumstances. When reversed this card prompts you to acknowledge any setbacks you're experiencing and confront the obstacles that are keeping you from moving on. It signifies a need to reassess your situation and find ways to overcome the hurdles that are hindering your progress.

A reversed Six of Swords serves as a reminder to be patient and open to adapting your plans. It encourages you to consider whether the current circumstances are truly conducive to change or if it's wiser to accept the status quo for now. By embracing a realistic view of your situation, you can make informed decisions and ultimately find a way to navigate through challenges with greater wisdom and perseverance.

SEVEN of SWORDS

◆

DECEPTION, SNEAKINESS, DISHONESTY

You stealthily fly under the radar, escaping in the night, convinced you've gotten away with something – but did you actually get away with it? Look carefully for the tiny people in the castle behind you: they see you, and they're going to call you out. On the other hand, perhaps it's not you who needs to be held accountable; maybe someone in your life is sneaking around and you need to be extra vigilant. Either way, it's a call for transparency. Whether you're getting called out or need to call someone else out, it's time to get brutally honest and reflect on what changes need to be made. There's no better time than now.

REVERSED

TRANSPARENCY, HONESTY, CONSCIENCE

A reversed Seven of Swords suggests a turning away from deception and manipulation, opting for a more straightforward approach. It prompts you to embrace integrity and act in alignment with your values, and signifies a willingness to be open and transparent in your interactions, choosing to uphold honesty over deceit.

This card serves as a reminder to confront any ethical dilemmas and choose the path that aligns with your conscience. It encourages you to take responsibility for your actions and prioritize authenticity in your dealings. By practicing transparency and owning up to your intentions, you can cultivate trust and maintain healthier relationships. A reversed Seven of Swords invites you to leave behind deceitful tactics and instead engage in interactions guided by genuine communication and ethical choices.

EIGHT of SWORDS

♦

SELF-SABOTAGE, SELF-DEFEAT, PERCEIVED POWERLESSNESS

The Eight of Swords challenges you to give up what no longer serves you. The woman is bound and blindfolded, bookended by eight swords that seem to block her movement. However, you might wonder whether the swords are really holding her back: can't she move forward? It looks as though she could escape the rope and take off her blindfold if she wanted to, and although it may take a little work she has more control over the situation than she realizes. That's what this card is all about: you may have found yourself in a prison of your own making, limiting your growth and progress by sticking to outdated beliefs and behavioral patterns that don't serve your higher good.

> ### AUTHOR'S NOTE
>
> Traditionally, the woman is surrounded by a pool of water, which represents her intuition: she'll need to tap into it to determine her next steps. Here I've incorporated this idea by giving some water-like, loose waves to her hair, tamed for now by the blindfold but waiting to be set free and wild when she's ready.

REVERSED

FREEDOM, EMPOWERMENT, SELF-RELIANCE

A reversed Eight of Swords signifies a breakthrough from self-imposed limitations and a newfound sense of liberation. The figure's unbound posture reflects a release from the entanglements that previously held them back. It prompts you to recognize your own power and potential, to take control of your circumstances and break free from the mental constraints that once hindered you.

This card reversed serves as a reminder to trust in your abilities and embrace self-reliance. It encourages you to step out of your comfort zone and seize opportunities for growth. By acknowledging your own agency and facing challenges with confidence, you can navigate life's obstacles with greater ease. It invites you to step into a new chapter of empowerment, and chart your own course toward personal fulfillment and independence.

NINE of SWORDS

◆

ANXIETY, DEPRESSION, FEAR

The Nine of Swords deals with what keeps you up at night: nervousness, insomnia, nightmares. The swords lined up above the bed symbolize her worries, one after another, which create a seemingly endless line-up of things to fear. This card calls you to acknowledge your feelings and be kind to yourself. It's not a time for toxic positivity or looking on the bright side, but you do need to take care of your physical and emotional health the best you can. Lean on your support network and enlist a trusted friend, family member, or therapist to help you talk through what scares you. Anxiety is a tricky thing, but sometimes when you shed light on your fears it robs them of their power.

> **AUTHOR'S NOTE**
>
> I illustrated this card and wrote this post in a holiday season during the COVID-19 pandemic that was rough in so many ways and on so many people. I wanted to acknowledge people who experience depression and anxiety around the holidays or deal with grief and other complicated emotions triggered by that time of year, especially when many of us were feeling isolated from the things and people we love the most.

REVERSED

RECOVERY, COPING MECHANISMS, HEALING

A reversed Nine of Swords offers a shift away from overwhelming anxiety and fear toward a period of gradual emotional restoration. It prompts you to acknowledge your progress in overcoming difficult thoughts and experiences, and signifies a time to implement healthier coping strategies and seek support in your journey towards healing.

This card reversed serves as a reminder to be kind to yourself and prioritize self-care as you navigate the process of recovery. It encourages you to explore positive outlets and resources that promote mental and emotional well-being. By working through your challenges and embracing strategies for healing, you can gradually find relief and regain a sense of inner peace.

TEN of SWORDS

◆

BLUNT ENDING, BETRAYAL, RESILIENCE

The Ten of Swords is a rough card to look at and can be alarming when you pull it, but no tarot card is a bad card. It represents a blunt ending of a romantic relationship, career, or friendship that damages your ability to trust. In the background, though, there's a sense that hope is on the horizon, that maybe this brutal ending needed to happen so a better opportunity could find its way into your life. It's a card of survival and resilience: you've been through a seemingly impossible life event and are bruised and battered, but wiser.

AUTHOR'S NOTE

I don't want to promote depictions of women as victims of violence, so it was difficult for me to illustrate this card with a woman victim for this women-led deck. In the Rider-Waite-Smith tarot the Ten of Swords shows a man laying face down with 10 swords stabbed in his back. My interpretation shows the woman facing up because I wanted to give her a sense of dignity and agency, and the impression that she might pull the swords out and break free.

REVERSED
REHABILITATION, STRENGTH, REBIRTH

A reversed Ten of Swords suggests a turning point away from the depths of pain and despair toward a period of renewal and resilience. When turned upside down you can imagine that gravity helps pull the swords away from her body and sets her on a path forward to physical and emotional healing. It prompts you to recognize your inner strength and rise above adversity with newfound determination. You are encouraged to let go of past wounds and embrace the opportunity to rebuild your life with greater wisdom and fortitude. By harnessing your inner strength and viewing challenges as stepping stones to growth, you can emerge from difficult times with a sense of empowerment and a renewed sense of purpose.

PAGE of SWORDS

◆

APPRENTICESHIP, GROWTH, ENTHUSIASM

The Page of Swords is ready to take on the world. She's fierce and determined, and approaches new projects with ferocious enthusiasm and optimism. She doesn't know what she doesn't know yet, and she's committed to learning and handling any potential obstacles along the way. As a young page she's going to make mistakes – that's par for the course when anyone takes on a different challenge – but she won't let herself get defeated by mistakes. She dusts herself off, gains valuable experience, and keeps moving and growing.

The Page of Swords embodies the spirit of apprenticeship, growth, and enthusiastic exploration. Depicted as a young girl holding a sword, honing her craft, this card symbolizes a fresh and curious approach to learning and discovery. In this spirit this card encourages you to embrace a beginner's mindset, approaching challenges with a willingness to learn. It represents a phase of intellectual growth where you're excited to expand your horizons and sharpen your analytical thinking.

REVERSED

INERTIA, DISINTEREST, INDIFFERENCE

A reversed Page of Swords suggests that the page's usual curiosity and enthusiasm may be dampened or misdirected. It could indicate a lack of engagement or reluctance to explore new ideas and experiences, and prompts you to assess whether you've become complacent or closed off to learning. It's a reminder to be cautious of apathy or a tendency to dismiss opportunities for growth.

This card also warns against engaging in gossip or spreading misinformation, as the page's penchant for curiosity might lead to a lack of discernment. It encourages you to be wary of making hasty judgments and consider the consequences of your words and actions. By actively seeking out fresh experiences, reigniting your curiosity, and approaching situations with a renewed sense of engagement, you can overcome inertia and re-embrace the page's spirit of discovery.

KNIGHT of SWORDS

◆

BOLDNESS, ASSERTIVENESS, DETERMINATION

The Knight of Swords is hyper-determined, sometimes to the point of tunnel vision. She is bold and assertive, doesn't take "No" for an answer, and uses her intellect to plan ahead and make her dreams reality. Nothing stands in her way: through rough winds and stormy seas, she gets where she needs to go. The Knight of Swords embodies a dynamic fusion of boldness, assertiveness, and determination. Depicted charging forward on her horse with a raised sword, she symbolizes a swift and unyielding pursuit of goals. This card represents the spirit of action, encouraging you to fearlessly confront challenges and seize opportunities with confidence.

The Knight of Swords signifies the need to approach situations with a strategic and assertive mindset, cutting through obstacles with unwavering determination. Her energy is a call to stand up for what you believe in and take calculated risks to achieve your ambitions. However, it's essential to balance this enthusiasm with thoughtful consideration, avoiding impulsive decisions that may overlook crucial details.

REVERSED

PASSIVITY, DISTRACTION, LACK OF VISION

A reversed Knight of Swords suggests that the knight's assertive and determined qualities might be stifled or misguided. It could indicate a tendency to lose focus or become easily distracted, hindering progress on your goals. This card reversed prompts you to re-evaluate your approach and consider whether impulsive actions are clouding your judgment, and is a reminder to be cautious of charging into situations without a well-defined plan as this may lead to fruitless efforts. This card also highlights the need to assess whether you're using your energy effectively or scattering it across various pursuits. By regaining a sense of direction, finding focus, and approaching challenges with strategic intent, you can overcome passivity and rekindle the knight's determined spirit to achieve more purposeful outcomes.

QUEEN of SWORDS

◆

LOGIC, CURIOSITY, DIRECT COMMUNICATION

The Queen of Swords leads with her head, not with her heart. She seeks to understand situations by examining them objectively and formulating plans based on logic and reason rather than emotions. She's surrounded by wind, representing change, and releases butterflies as a sign of transformation. Her sword signifies swift, decisive action, and confidence in her decisions. She embodies qualities of clear communication, logic, and discernment and is unafraid to confront truths, both within herself and the world around her. Her wisdom is balanced by a firm yet compassionate demeanor.

This card signifies a person who can cut through illusions and see situations objectively, making well-informed decisions based on intellect. While her approach may come across as detached, it stems from a desire to protect and guide. The Queen of Swords encourages honesty, directness, and the pursuit of knowledge. When this card appears, it often suggests a need to harness your analytical abilities and maintain a balance between rational thinking and compassionate understanding.

REVERSED

ANIMOSITY, INDECISIVENESS, LACK OF SELF-CONFIDENCE

A reversed Queen of Swords signifies a potential imbalance in communication, intellect, or emotional expression. You or someone in your life may be taking action or making decisions based purely on emotion, not logic. This reversal can suggest a tendency toward overly harsh judgments, cutting remarks, or emotional detachment, and might indicate a need to avoid being overly critical or rigid in your thinking. When reversed it prompts you to assess any areas where you might be lacking in empathy, and can suggest a need to guard against manipulative behavior or dishonesty. While an upright Queen of Swords embodies wisdom and clarity, the reversed position encourages you to seek a more balanced integration of your intellect and emotions, fostering compassionate communication and understanding. By striving for a harmonious blend of thoughtfulness and empathy, you can navigate challenges with grace and create more meaningful connections.

KING of SWORDS

◆

POWER, IMPARTIALITY, ACCOMPLISHMENT

The King of Swords relies on her strength, skill, and experience to rule her kingdom with fairness, reason, and impartiality. She takes her responsibilities seriously and commits to making positive changes that benefit communities. Her butterflies represent change and transformation. This card represents a figure of authority, intellect, and decisive leadership who is known for her ability to make impartial judgments and provide practical solutions to complex issues. She upholds strong moral principles and encourages others to do the same.

The King of Swords often symbolizes a person who has achieved mastery in their field and can provide guidance and wisdom to others. It encourages critical thinking, strategic planning, and effective decision-making. When this card appears it may suggest the need to approach situations with a rational mindset, relying on knowledge and experience to navigate challenges. It also underscores the importance of seeking truth, maintaining integrity, and using your intellect to lead and inspire those around you.

REVERSED
BIAS, MANIPULATION, INJUSTICE

The King of Swords reversed suggests that the qualities of logic and fairness associated with the card may be compromised. It could point to a misuse of power or authority, where decisions are driven by personal agenda rather than objective analysis. When reversed this card warns against being swayed by manipulation or succumbing to deceitful tactics, and highlights the need to be cautious of individuals who may exploit their knowledge or position for personal gain. It prompts you to examine your own motivations and actions, ensuring you're approaching situations with transparency and integrity. It also serves as a reminder to challenge your biases and preconceptions to avoid contributing to unjust outcomes. Reversed, the King of Swords underscores the importance of seeking truth, uncovering hidden motives, and upholding principles of honesty and fairness in all endeavors.

ACE of PENTACLES

◆

POTENTIAL, OPPORTUNITIES, MANIFESTATION

The aces of a tarot deck represent new beginnings, fresh opportunities, and lots of potential. For the Ace of Pentacles this means potential for financial and material wealth in your life, but it's not a guarantee. You need to be open to opportunities that come your way, and you need to jump on those opportunities when you see them. This card prompts you to recognize and seize the opportunities that are presenting themselves in your life. It signifies a time to embark on ventures that have the potential to yield tangible and practical results.

The Ace of Pentacles serves as a reminder to harness your skills and resources to manifest your goals and desires. It encourages you to invest your energy in and focus on endeavors that align with your values and ambitions. By nurturing the seeds of potential with determination and practicality, you can lay the foundation for long-term success and material well-being. The Ace of Pentacles invites you to embrace the possibilities before you and work toward manifesting your aspirations in the physical realm.

REVERSED

SHORTSIGHTEDNESS, INDECISION, MISSED OPPORTUNITIES

A reversed Ace of Pentacles suggests a temporary blockage in the flow of abundance and material growth. The pentacle held upside down symbolizes a lack of readiness to seize opportunities. When reversed this card prompts you to reflect on any missed chances or hesitations that may be hindering your progress. It signifies a need to address any indecisiveness or lack of clarity that's preventing you from fully embracing opportunities that are offered to you. Consider reassessing your goals and examine whether your current path aligns with your long-term ambitions. This could be the perfect time to address potential limitations, and set yourself on a path toward growth.

TWO of PENTACLES

◆

MULTITASKING, AGILITY, ADAPTABILITY

The Two of Pentacles represents multitasking and prioritization: one hand's full and she opens her other hand to accept more. She's handling lots of tasks and issues with skill, agility, and grace and makes her efforts look easy, but as we all know it takes a lot of work to make things look simple. This card is a reminder to take care of yourself so you don't burn out, and to make sure to delegate tasks when needed.

The Two of Pentacles signifies the ability to handle various responsibilities with finesse, balance, and a sense of self-awareness, of knowing your own limits and boundaries. It prompts you to embrace your capacity to navigate diverse tasks and situations and signifies a time of versatility and effective time management, allowing you to address multiple priorities with ease.

REVERSED

BURNOUT, OVERWORK, INFLEXIBILITY

A reversed Two of Pentacles points to an imbalance and struggle to juggle multiple responsibilities. When flipped upside down it becomes more awkward to catch the pentacles in her hands as they head toward the ground, which could represent a lack of harmony and stability.

When reversed this card prompts you to recognize the toll that excessive demands and rigid routines may be taking on your well-being. It signifies a need to address the patterns of overwork and inflexibility that are leading to burnout. Remember that you don't need to be everywhere all at once, or be everything to everybody: this is an impossible task to expect of anyone, and you are no exception. Give yourself some grace and map out your priorities to determine where your efforts are best directed. Take this as a sign to prioritize self-care and seek ways to restore balance in your life. By embracing flexibility and allowing yourself moments of rest, you can navigate challenges with greater ease. A reversed Two of Pentacles invites you to make adjustments to prevent burnout and foster a healthier and more harmonious approach to managing your obligations.

THREE of PENTACLES

◆

TEAMWORK, COLLABORATION, FUTURE PLANNING

The Three of Pentacles represents a particularly fruitful time for productive teamwork and collaboration. The *Black Violet Tarot*'s interpretation of this idea depicts three women working together to collect grapes, perhaps to include in a dinner celebration or to make wine. Whatever their plans are, they listen to each other respectfully and enthusiastically. They're excited to work on this project and enjoy their time together. Everyone gets a say in the process, hand selecting the best grapes for the job and strategically planning their next steps for future harvests.

REVERSED

EGO, CONFLICT, MISCOMMUNICATION

When reversed, the grapes the women are collecting turn to – you might have guessed it – sour grapes. Suddenly there's jealousy, miscommunication, and over-inflated egos. This reversal suggests a disruption in collaboration and a breakdown in effective teamwork. Maybe each collaborator is taking more than their fair share, or maybe they're each competing to grab all the credit for everyone's work. Either way, there's more of a focus on individual accomplishment than a collaborative, community effort.

A reversed Three of Pentacles prompts you to address any ego-driven tendencies or misunderstandings that are hindering cooperation. It signifies a need to confront conflicts and communication barriers that are preventing successful collaboration. Put aside individual agendas and egos in favor of a shared goal. It also encourages you to engage in open dialogue and clarify expectations to avoid misunderstandings.

FOUR of PENTACLES

◆

MISERLINESS, DISCONNECTION, SELF-CENTEREDNESS

The Four of Pentacles asks you to reflect on your relationship with money. You may have accumulated wealth over your lifetime, but is it making you happy? The woman holds tightly to the pentacle in her hand, and stands close to the three beside her. She has walled herself off to safeguard her earnings, but it has come to the point where she can't move. She's restricted by her focus on material wealth, unable to enjoy the sun that shines above her head and the beauty of nature that surrounds her. Even the cloak she wears obscures her face, further impeding her ability to connect with people in a meaningful way. Think Ebenezer Scrooge from *A Christmas Carol* before his visits from the three ghosts.

REVERSED

GENEROSITY, OPENNESS OR RECKLESS SPENDING, WASTEFULNESS

You may notice that when the Four of Pentacles is reversed the pentacles seem as though they could drop out of the woman's hands and out of the ravine she's in. This card reversed is just that: a release of material possessions, and a boost in willingness to share resources with others. It prompts you to embrace a more open-hearted approach to both giving and receiving, and signifies a time to let go of rigid attachment to possessions and be more willing to contribute to the well-being of others.

A balance can be struck between financial responsibility and the enjoyment of life's pleasures. The Four of Pentacles reversed encourages you to avoid wastefulness, while also avoiding excessive stinginess. By adopting a more open and generous mindset, you can foster deeper connections and experience greater satisfaction in sharing your resources. When reversed it invites you to explore the rewards of giving and enjoying life's abundance without becoming reckless or overly indulgent.

FIVE of PENTACLES

◆

HARDSHIP, ISOLATION, POVERTY

The Five of Pentacles represents a time of hardship and isolation. The woman walks alone in sadness, enduring the wind and snow. She feels as though she doesn't have anyone to turn to for help. She's passing by a stained glass window, presumably a church, where people are known to congregate together as a community, but for whatever reason she feels overlooked by and separated from this community, and can't look to them for help or support.

As a minor arcana card – which deal with ever-changing, everyday life events – know that this period of loneliness and struggle is temporary. Eventually she will find her way out of this and find her people. This is a card of hope for anyone feeling isolated and alone.

REVERSED

FORGIVENESS, BELONGING, OVERCOMING HARDSHIP

A reversed Five of Pentacles signifies a shift from a sense of exclusion and hardship towards finding solace and healing. It prompts you to embrace the power of forgiveness and seek reconciliation with those you may have felt disconnected from, and invites you to let go of past grievances and work toward rebuilding bonds.

Even in times of adversity, there is the potential for healing and reintegration. This reversal encourages you to reach out to others and seek the support and connections you need to overcome isolation. By extending forgiveness and embracing a renewed sense of belonging, you can transform challenging experiences into opportunities for growth and connection. A reversed Five of Pentacles invites you to move beyond isolation and towards a more harmonious and supportive environment.

SIX of PENTACLES

♦

GENEROSITY, PHILANTHROPY, SOLIDARITY

The Six of Pentacles represents financial security and generosity. The woman on the right has accumulated enough wealth to be financially secure and is giving money to the woman on the left, who could use some help. This card serves as a reminder that life is a series of peaks and valleys: sometimes in life you need help, while at other times you're in a position to offer help.

The Pentacles suit represents finances, but giving can also and often does refer to emotional support. You may notice the wealthy woman is carrying a scale, symbolizing balance, which represents the need to avoid one-sided relationships where you're constantly giving without receiving, or vice versa.

> ### AUTHOR'S NOTE
>
> In the original Rider-Waite-Smith tarot the wealthy man is dropping coins into the hands of poor men. It was important to me that the two women were having a true interaction with each other: the wealthy woman places the coin into the poor woman's hand, rather than dropping it. This makes for a more compassionate interaction, and nods to the fact that their situations could easily be reversed.

REVERSED

SELF-CARE, INEQUALITY, DEBT

Every time we get on a plane we're reminded in the event of an emergency to adjust our oxygen masks before doing so for others. That's the idea behind the Six of Pentacles reversed: you can't give so much of yourself to others that you end up putting yourself in physical, mental, or financial jeopardy. Take an honest look at your capabilities, and how much energy or resources you can reasonably give to others without hurting yourself. This is an open invitation to prioritize your wellness and not spread yourself too thin. It can also be a nudge to take a hard look at your finances to see where you can improve your life through thoughtful budgeting and smarter investments.

> ### AUTHOR'S NOTE
>
> I decided to check my credit score after years of knowing that I had lousy credit. Knowledge is power, and the situation wasn't nearly as bad as had I thought it was. By taking the first, scary step of honestly looking at my finances I was able to figure out where I had gone wrong, and put myself on a path to repairing it.

SEVEN of PENTACLES

◆

PERSEVERANCE, STABILITY, INVESTMENT

The Seven of Pentacles shows a woman who has earned and saved for a long time, and takes a step back to look at what she has built. She grew this tree from a seedling, and it now stands tall and blooms with pentacles. She takes one pentacle for her immediate needs, and saves the rest for the future. This card takes a big-picture view of financial planning, and suggests you're in or about to start a period of building financial stability. Alternatively, you may have already amassed a significant nest egg.

REVERSED

PROCRASTINATION, IMMODERATION, LACK OF PLANNING

A reversed Seven of Pentacles indicates a departure from the careful cultivation of resources depicted in the upright version of the card. The woman's delayed action and disregard for moderation reflect a missed opportunity to continue nurturing her growth. In this card the woman's hesitation to take action suggests a tendency toward procrastination: instead of reaping the rewards of her careful planning, she may find herself facing setbacks due to a lack of timely effort. The card also highlights a lack of moderation and impulsive decision-making. Rather than wisely saving and investing her hard-earned pentacles, the woman may indulge in imprudent spending, leading to financial instability. Furthermore, a reversed Seven of Pentacles underscores the importance of planning and foresight. Without a clear strategy, the woman risks undermining the stability she worked hard to build.

Overall, a reversed Seven of Pentacles serves as a cautionary tale against complacency, impulsivity, and inadequate planning. It encourages you to stay committed to your financial goals, make timely and thoughtful decisions, and avoid short-sighted actions that could jeopardize your long-term stability.

EIGHT of PENTACLES

◆

GROWTH, APPRENTICESHIP, PRACTICE

The Eight of Pentacles is a card of learning and apprenticeship. Fully immersed in her work, the woman voluntarily isolates herself and removes distractions so she can fully dedicate her time and concentration to building her skills. Her actions are repetitive; she's committed to practicing until she's a master of her craft. This card represents a period of growth and development where your commitment to honing your abilities will lead to mastery. Just as the woman painstakingly creates each pentacle, your focus on details and a willingness to put in the effort required will pay off. This card suggests you're in a phase of concentrated learning, where the accumulation of knowledge and experience will ultimately contribute to your success. Embrace this time of apprenticeship, be patient with yourself, and know that your dedication will lead to significant progress and accomplishment.

REVERSED

PERFECTIONISM, OVERTHINKING, FRUSTRATION

A reversed Eight of Pentacles indicates the woman's dedication to her craft has become a source of stress and self-doubt, leading to a sense of dissatisfaction rather than accomplishment. While the upright card symbolized growth through steady effort, when reversed it suggests that your pursuit of mastery might be marred by a tendency toward perfectionism. Instead of embracing the learning process, you may find yourself getting caught up in details and striving for an unattainable level of perfection.

Overthinking and self-criticism can cloud your progress. Don't hold yourself to unfair expectations, and don't let your craft become a mental burden that hampers your ability to learn, improve, and grow. While mastery is a noble goal, it's important to enjoy the learning process and acknowledge that growth involves imperfection. By addressing perfectionist tendencies and easing self-imposed pressures, you can cultivate a healthier and more fulfilling approach to your pursuits.

NINE of PENTACLES

◆

CONTENTMENT, PRIDE, WISDOM

The Nine of Pentacles is about enjoying the fruits (literally: look at the grapes!) of your hard-earned labor. The woman has worked hard and has built a life that allows her security and comfort, and she never takes those for granted. Getting to this point has required tenacity, along with an ability to roll with the punches, celebrate wins, and learn from failures. She's had to be fearless in going after what she wants and needs. Her falcon (think: falconry) represents her ability to skillfully discover and hunt down opportunities that spark emotional, intellectual, and material growth. She's built up quite the archive of experiences, and she can pass along her wisdom to others.

REVERSED

INSTABILITY, DISSATISFACTION, LONGING

A reversed Nine of Pentacles offers a contrasting perspective to the upright meaning, for now the woman's sense of contentment and security becomes fragile and the once-abundant grapes symbolize a feeling of scarcity. While the upright card symbolized enjoying the rewards of hard work, when reversed this card suggests a temporary state of instability. Dissatisfaction may stem from a longing for something more, or a recognition that material wealth alone doesn't bring lasting fulfillment. The woman's gaze suggests a yearning for a deeper sense of purpose or connection.

A reversed card also underscores the impermanence of external achievements. What once brought pride and comfort now feels uncertain, prompting a re-evaluation of what truly matters. In this context, a reversed Nine of Pentacles invites you to explore your inner world and sources of fulfillment beyond material possessions. While challenges may arise, they offer an opportunity to reassess your priorities and find stability through inner growth and a broader sense of abundance.

TEN of PENTACLES

◆

SECURITY, LOVE, ROOTS

The Ten of Pentacles represents love, family, connections, and roots. The older woman has spent her life building a strong, solid foundation so that her family can grow in comfort and security. At this point she has everything she needs, and can generously offer support to her children and grandchildren. The future of her family is sustainable and full of promise. This card often represents the completion of an important, formative journey, where you're invited to take a moment to reflect on and enjoy your accomplishments.

REVERSED

CONFLICT, INSTABILITY, ISOLATION

A reversed Ten of Pentacles turns a harmonious family scene into one marked by discord and disconnection. While the upright card symbolized the culmination of a journey marked by security and love, when reversed it suggests upheaval within familial bonds. This reversal hints at underlying tensions and struggles. Conflict may arise as the once solid foundation crumbles, leading to a sense of instability and uncertainty among family members. Financial or emotional strains might contribute to the breakdown of relationships.

A reversed Ten of Pentacles invites you to address conflicts and disruptions within your familial or social circles. It's a reminder to nurture connections, communicate openly, and work toward resolving issues to restore a sense of stability and harmony. By acknowledging challenges and seeking reconciliation, you can work toward rebuilding a stronger and more connected foundation.

PAGE of PENTACLES

◆

STRATEGY, GROWTH, APPRENTICESHIP

The Page of Pentacles is at the beginning of her journey to building wealth, financial stability, and abundance. She holds the pentacle above her head as a way to visualize her goals, not in a way that's obsessed or greed driven but to keep her focused as she plans her strategy. She's excited to put one foot in front of the other to see where it leads.

The Page of Pentacles embodies the themes of strategy, growth, and apprenticeship. The young woman represents a diligent learner who approaches her endeavors with a thoughtful and strategic mindset. This card signifies a phase of focused learning and skill development, often related to practical matters or financial matters. She approaches her goals with a sense of responsibility and eagerness to expand her knowledge.

This card encourages you to explore new opportunities and invest time in honing your skills. It emphasizes the importance of setting a strong foundation for future success through careful, patient planning and a willingness to learn from others. By approaching her path with a strategic perspective, she can navigate challenges and opportunities with poise, setting the stage for future prosperity and accomplishment.

REVERSED

PROCRASTINATION, SHORT-TERM VISION, LACK OF PLANNING

A reversed Page of Pentacles may struggle with delayed action, and has a tendency to prioritize immediate gratification over long-term goals. Her inability to focus on strategic planning and skill development hinders her growth and potential. When reversed this card serves as a reminder that avoiding responsibility and neglecting learning opportunities can lead to missed chances for progress. This card prompts you to address a habit of short-term thinking and develop a more disciplined approach. It encourages you to be mindful of the value of investing time and effort in building a solid foundation for future success, ultimately leading to a more fulfilling and prosperous journey.

KNIGHT of PENTACLES

◆

EARNESTNESS, DETERMINATION, CONCENTRATION

The Knight of Pentacles is serious and determined. She sets her short- and long-term goals and takes practical, methodical steps to achieve them. Her path is slow and calculated: she doesn't let herself get sidetracked by nonsense or naysayers. She's confident in her abilities and knows she'll get where she needs to be on her own timeline. The woman holds a pentacle while walking through the woods, and exemplifies a diligent approach to her goals. This card signifies a person who is committed to achieving their objectives through dedicated effort.

The Knight of Pentacles highlights the importance of persistent and sustained effort, encouraging you to continue moving forward with your plans despite any obstacles. It reflects an individual who is willing to invest time and energy in their pursuits, fostering a sense of responsibility and reliability. By embodying the qualities of earnestness, concentration, and determination, you can navigate challenges with resilience and lay the foundation for lasting success.

REVERSED
BEING A SPENDTHRIFT, RISK TAKING WITH MONEY AND STABILITY, POOR FINANCIAL DECISIONS

The impulsive nature of the reversed Knight of Pentacles leads her to make poor choices that jeopardize stability and long-term security. Rather than employing a cautious and disciplined approach to managing resources, she may engage in hasty spending or speculative investments. Her tendency to prioritize short-term gratification over long-term sustainability can lead to instability and financial challenges. When reversed this card serves as a reminder to exercise prudence, research thoroughly before making decisions, and prioritize financial responsibility. It suggests a need to rein in impulsivity and adopt a more strategic outlook on money matters. By recognizing the importance of balanced financial management and curbing unnecessary risk taking, you can work toward achieving greater stability and security in your financial endeavors.

QUEEN of PENTACLES

◆

MATRIARCHY, BREADWINNING, CARETAKING

The Queen of Pentacles is a maternal, nurturing figure who takes care of her loved ones emotionally and financially. She's a breadwinner, and her ability to balance work and home life seems effortless, but it's not: it takes a lot of effort to make things look easy. However, caring and providing for herself and others is a true labor of love for her, and she'd prefer to live no other way. Depicted as a nurturing figure surrounded by nature, she symbolizes a strong, grounded presence who balances practicality with compassion, ensuring the well-being of her family and community.

The Queen of Pentacles excels at creating a comfortable and nurturing environment. She's adept at managing material and emotional resources, and takes pride in her ability to provide stability and security. This card reflects a harmonious blend of practicality and sensibility, emphasizing the importance of using your resources wisely and nurturing those around you. The Queen of Pentacles has an innate ability to excel in homemaking and professional endeavors. Her energy encourages you to prioritize self-sufficiency, take charge of your responsibilities, and create a warm and nurturing atmosphere for yourself and others.

> ### AUTHOR'S NOTE
> The little rabbit jumping in the corner is a symbol of fertility and abundance, two concepts held dear by the Queen of Pentacles.

REVERSED
GREED, SELFISHNESS OR, MORE POSITIVELY, FINANCIAL INDEPENDENCE

This card reversed suggests that the nurturing and practical qualities associated with the Queen of Pentacles may be distorted or imbalanced. It could indicate a preoccupation with material wealth and possessions, potentially leading to neglect of emotional and spiritual needs. On a more positive note, when reversed this card may also highlight a growing emphasis on financial independence and self-sufficiency, and could signify a period of focused effort toward achieving financial stability or pursuing personal goals. It prompts you to ensure your pursuits align with your values and well-being. This card reversed encourages you to find balance between material wealth and emotional fulfillment.

KING of PENTACLES

◆

LEADERSHIP, ABUNDANCE, PROSPERITY

The King of Pentacles leads her kingdom into an era of security and abundance. She works hard and strategically to ensure her citizens (as opposed to "subjects") have everything they need in order to thrive, such as food to eat and a safe place to live. She's just and a true advocate of the people. The King of Pentacles is a symbol of financial security and accomplishment. This card reflects a blend of practicality and generosity, emphasizing the importance of achieving success while also enriching other people's lives. With this card there is a balance between work and reward, and discipline and enjoyment. Her energy encourages you to take charge of your financial endeavors, make sound investments, and create a life of comfort and stability. This card will inspire you to embrace your potential for prosperity and share your blessings with others.

> ### AUTHOR'S NOTE
>
> The Rider-Waite-Smith card shows the King of Pentacles sitting on a throne adorned with bull sculptures. My version nods to this idea by making the king a little bull-like, with a tiny nose ring and the sides of her crown resembling a bull's horns.

REVERSED

SELFISHNESS, INCOMPETENCE, SCARCITY

A reversal of this card suggests the king's qualities of abundance and mastery may be distorted or lacking. It could indicate a self-serving attitude, where personal gain takes precedence over the well-being of others. She might display a lack of competence in financial matters or leadership. This card prompts you to assess whether selfish motivations or a lack of understanding are hindering your ability to effectively lead or manage resources. On a positive note, a reversed card can also reflect a growing awareness of the importance of addressing a scarcity mindset and learning to value abundance in both material and emotional aspects of life. By acknowledging areas of improvement, you can work towards cultivating a more balanced and generous approach, fostering both your own growth and that of those around you.

ACE of WANDS

◆

INSPIRATION, MOTIVATION, PASSION

The Ace of Wands is a card of inspiration and motivation, and encourages you to follow your passion. Have an idea for a new business venture, life change, or creative project? This card gives you the green light to get started on it, even if you just take a few baby steps to lay the groundwork. It will spark your imagination and push you to explore uncharted territories. Like a seed bursting forth from the earth, the Ace of Wands symbolizes the birth of new possibilities and the potential for incredible growth. Embrace this surge of energy, let it fuel your determination, and watch as your ideas take shape with a fervor that only genuine passion can provide.

REVERSED

DELAYS, CREATIVE BLOCKS, LACK OF INSPIRATION

In the reversed position the vibrant energy that usually accompanies this card may feel stifled, leaving you struggling to find the motivation to pursue your passions. It's as though the spark that once ignited your enthusiasm is casting a shadow over your creative endeavors. While setbacks are a natural part of any journey, they can also serve as opportunities for introspection and growth. Reassess your goals and explore the root causes of your creative stagnation. Delve into activities that reignite your inner flame, whether it's trying out new artistic media, seeking fresh sources of inspiration, or revisiting past triumphs. A reversed Ace of Wands suggests that this temporary phase will eventually give way to renewed motivation and fresh bursts of creativity.

AUTHOR'S NOTE

Take breaks when you need to: the work will still be there when you return, and sometimes all you need is to recharge physically and mentally to start being creative again. I went through a very emotional and exhausting period when creating *Black Violet Tarot*, and stopped writing and illustrating whenever I hit creative blocks. It took me almost three years to create this deck, but I strongly believe the output was so much better because I didn't push myself to create when I didn't feel inspired.

TWO of WANDS

♦

OPPORTUNITY, TURNING POINT, LEAP OF FAITH

The Two of Wands shows a woman with two wands: one inactive in her hand, and one tucked away in her pocket. She stares at a globe, contemplating where she could go, but doesn't take action. This card suggests you're on the verge of something – a new project, a career change, moving, or taking a trip somewhere different – but you're not quite ready to make the leap. Perhaps you haven't mapped out a plan, or you're afraid to leave your comfort zone.

This card embodies a pivotal turning point in your life. The woman's stance conveys a sense of anticipation, as if she stands at a crossroads of decisions. The inactive wand signifies untapped potential, while the globe signifies the vast world of possibilities. It encourages you to step beyond your boundaries and explore the uncharted territories that lie ahead.

Although uncertainty might linger, remember that great achievements often require embracing the unknown. With careful planning and a daring spirit, you can transform "What if" into "I did it."

REVERSED

RISK AVERSION, HESITATION, AVOIDANCE

In a reversed Two of Wands the woman's hesitation intensifies as she clings to her wands, apprehensive about stepping into the unknown. The globe in her hand seems like a daunting challenge rather than an exciting prospect. This card highlights an inner struggle with risk aversion and a tendency to avoid change. Despite standing at the precipice of opportunities, fear holds sway, hindering your progress. When reversed this card speaks the consequences of hesitating to make decisions and symbolizes stagnation, where the allure of comfort zones outweighs the allure of unexplored options. While caution has its place, overly hesitating can lead to missed chances for growth. Assess your fears and consider the balance between security and growth. Though uncertainty may persist, embracing calculated risks can lead to personal and professional development, fostering a path that ultimately bridges the gap between "What if" and "What could be."

THREE of WANDS

◆

FORESIGHT, STRATEGY, OPPORTUNITY

The Three of Wands suggests that major obstacles have lifted or are lifting from your path, putting you in a great position to embark on formative experiences. Even if your path won't be easy, you're at least in a place where you can foresee potential challenges and strategize your way around them well in advance. Things have been hard and good things don't always come easy, but you're going to be better equipped than ever to accomplish your goals.

The woman in the card stands with a sense of confidence, gazing ahead. The three wands symbolize the collaboration between past, present, and future endeavors. It's as though you've climbed a hill to gain a vantage point, allowing you to identify potential pitfalls and plot a course that navigates them effectively. The Three of Wands encourages you to trust in your abilities and utilize your learned wisdom to embrace upcoming challenges. By combining your insight with a well thought out plan, you're setting the stage for accomplishments that reflect your resilience and pave the way for lasting success.

REVERSED

CONTINUED OBSTACLES, DELAYS, PERSEVERANCE

When reversed the Three of Wands suggests that, despite the previous progress you have made, challenges still persist on your journey. The once-clear path may now seem clouded, causing frustration and impeding your forward momentum. However, while it may feel as though progress is slow or even halted, remember that enduring through adversity can build resilience and strength.

A reversed position encourages you to stay patient and persistent, even in the face of mounting difficulties. Re-evaluate your strategies and plans, seeking opportunities to overcome the hurdles that lie before you. It might be tempting to lose heart, but by summoning your determination you can navigate the complexities ahead. Your perseverance will eventually lead you to the rewards and achievements you've been working towards, proving that challenges, though daunting, can also be stepping stones towards greater accomplishments.

FOUR of WANDS

◆

HARMONY, CELEBRATION, STABILITY

The Four of Wands represents security and stability, returning you to familiar ground to celebrate your accomplishments with the people you love and trust the most. You've worked hard – struggled, even – and all that work is finally paying off in tangible ways. It's time to enjoy the fruits of your labor and take pride that you've gotten yourself to this place. Representing growth and expansion, this card depicts two sets of twins to illustrate the idea of doubling or multiplying. You've come a long way and have worked tirelessly to build something out of nothing. Take the time to celebrate your accomplishments before continuing on your journey.

The Four of Wands radiates with themes of harmony and celebration. It encourages you to bask in this moment of harmony, acknowledging the stability you've created and relishing the shared celebrations that fortify your connections.

REVERSED
ABANDONMENT. CONFLICT. DISCONNECTION

In the reversed position the Four of Wands takes on a different tone, embodying themes of abandonment, conflict, and disconnection. The once-harmonious scene depicted by the upright card now reflects a sense of disarray and disruption. The celebratory atmosphere has faded, giving way to discord and tension. This card serves as a reminder that sometimes even amid accomplishments, misunderstandings or conflicts can arise, leading to a sense of isolation.

When reversed it suggests a temporary rupture in the bonds that were once strong. It might signify a period of feeling disconnected from the support network you once relied upon, leaving you to navigate challenges without the familiar sense of unity. Use this reversal as an opportunity to address the conflicts that have arisen and seek resolutions that can help mend the fractured connections. While the reversal may signify a period of turmoil, it also highlights the potential for growth and understanding that can come from addressing and reconciling the issues at hand.

FIVE of WANDS

◆

CONFLICT, CONFUSION, CHAOS

The fives in tarot generally refer to discord and disruption, and the Five of Wands is no exception. When you pull this card, think about what area in your life generates the most conflict. Is that conflict leading anywhere productive, or does it just cause unnecessary chaos and confusion? Conflict can be a good or bad thing. Good conflict = finding yourself in a work environment full of diverse, talented minds that don't always see eye to eye, but can battle it out productively in a boardroom or debate. Bad conflict = causing arguments for the sake of arguments, talking without listening, and toxic friendships.

You'll see hands holding wands in a way you'd see someone holding knives or ice picks. They're ready for a fight but they're not actually hitting anyone with their wands, which suggests that the conflict is unnecessary. Everyone involved needs to work through it or get away from it.

REVERSED
TRUCE, PEACE, COMPROMISE

A reversed Five of Wands signifies a shift from conflict to truce, and from chaos to compromise. The hands that once held wands like weapons are now lowering them, indicating a cessation of hostilities and a desire for resolution. This card invites you to break free from the cycle of strife and seek harmony through understanding and cooperation. In contrast to the upright depiction of discord, when reversed this card embodies the potential for finding common ground. It encourages you to assess whether ongoing conflicts serve any productive purpose or whether they're merely causing unnecessary turmoil. This card emphasizes the importance of choosing battles wisely and working towards beneficial resolutions.

Embrace the energy of this card as a reminder that conflicts can transform into opportunities for growth and connection when approached with an open mind and a willingness to find middle ground. By striving for peaceful solutions and genuine compromise, you can dismantle the barriers that fueled the chaos depicted in the upright Five of Wands.

SIX of WANDS

♦

SUCCESS, CONFIDENCE, RECOGNITION

The Six of Wands is a card of confidence gained through hard knocks. You've had your nose to the grindstone for a long time, soaking up information like a sponge and building your skills through trial and error, determination, and grit. You've seen and learned things, and now you know things. You're ready and more than capable of succeeding at anything you set your mind to. People around you recognize you for your knowledge and talents and will often seek you out for advice or feedback on whatever they're working on. Celebrate your success and share your knowledge freely with others, but make sure to take care of yourself and set up appropriate boundaries.

The figure riding the horse is adorned with a laurel wreath as a symbol of achievement. You can imagine she's galloping toward a cheering crowd, giving her the acknowledgment and respect she has earned through hard work. This card encourages you to revel in your accomplishments, allowing the recognition to fuel your continued growth. Remember that sharing your wisdom can inspire others to follow in your footsteps, forging a legacy of success and empowerment.

REVERSED

SELF-RECOGNITION, PERSONAL GAIN OR
LACK OF RECOGNITION/REWARDS

A reversed Six of Wands suggest that, despite your efforts and achievements, there might be a sense of internal validation that takes precedence over seeking approval from others. You've embarked on a journey of self-discovery, honing your skills, yet the need for external recognition might feel diminished. This card prompts you to reflect on your motivations and whether your accomplishments align with your personal goals.

In contrast with the cheering crowd depicted in the upright card, this card reversed might signify a quiet form of success, where the rewards are more intrinsic than public. While others may not fully appreciate your achievements, it's essential to recognize your accomplishments and self-worth. Whether or not the world sees your achievements, your journey is ultimately about your growth and fulfillment.

SEVEN of WANDS

◆

PROTECTION, ENVY, CHALLENGE

The Seven of Wands is about speaking your mind even if your voice shakes, as it symbolizes self-defense and self-protection in the face of aggressive competition. You've worked hard to achieve success and are now in a coveted position, and many people envy what you have and want to be where you are. The woman is confronted by a group of competitors aiming to take her place, and even though she feels as though she's fighting on uneven ground she's ready to take on the challenge and defend her territory.

This card captures the essence of standing up for yourself, facing challenges, and navigating envy. The wand raised as a weapon signifies her willingness to defend her achievements. The Seven of Wands encourages you to hold your ground, even if the odds seem stacked against you. Your determination and resilience can serve as powerful tools for safeguarding what you've earned. Trust in your abilities, speak your truth, and let your inner strength shine through, proving that you're ready to face any challenge head on.

REVERSED

BURNOUT, SURRENDER, SELF-CENSORSHIP

This card reversed suggests that the constant struggle depicted in the upright card has taken a toll, and you might find yourself feeling overwhelmed by the demands of protecting your position. The need to defend and fight off challenges may have led to exhaustion, making it difficult to sustain the battle.

In contrast with the resolute stance of the upright version, a reversed Seven of Wands suggests a need to reassess your approach. You may feel as though you're fighting an uphill battle that's draining your energy and creativity, which is a sign that self-care and acknowledging your limits are crucial. This card encourages you to let go of the need to constantly prove your worth. Surrendering the need for unending vigilance can allow you to find a more balanced approach, preserving your well-being and preventing burnout. Embrace self-compassion and consider where it's time to ease up, redirect your energy, and foster a healthier sense of equilibrium.

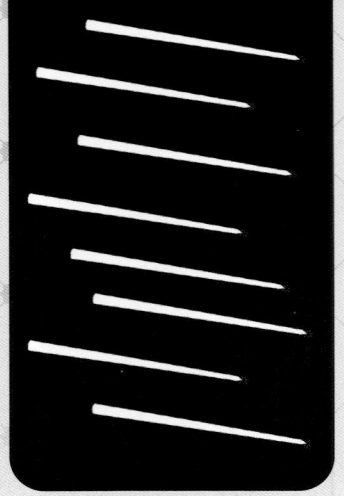

EIGHT of WANDS

◆

PROGRESS, CHANGE, SPEED

The Eight of Wands signals a period when you're able to move forward quickly, and with a clear focus, toward your goals. It's a very fertile time to make change happen if you want it to. Don't be afraid to progress: you've worked hard and overcome a lot to get to this point, and you've earned the chance to build what you've been dreaming of.

The wands fly through the air like arrows, representing the swift momentum of your endeavors. The obstacles that once hindered you are now dissipating, allowing your intentions to soar toward fruition. This card encourages you to take advantage of the momentum, and trust the path you're on. Your dedication and resilience have paved the way for this period of acceleration, and as you navigate the change remember that the energy of the wands is propelling you forward. Keep your focus sharp, and enjoy the exhilarating journey of transformation.

REVERSED

DELAYS, BARRIERS, SETBACKS

When reversed this card indicates a slowing down and halt in the momentum represented by its upright counterpart. The arrows that once shot forward with speed now seem suspended, as though caught in mid-air. This card signifies a time when the swift movement toward your goals is impeded.

Contrary to the rapid change of the upright card, the reversed version suggests a period of stagnation or uncertainty. Plans might be put on hold, and the clear focus you once had may become muddled. It's essential to be patient and adaptable during this time. While the energy of progress might be temporarily obstructed, remember that periods of pause can also provide opportunities for reflection and recalibration. Change isn't always linear, and setbacks can lead to valuable insights. As you navigate the challenges presented by the reversed Eight of Wands, consider how you can re-evaluate your strategies and maintain your determination even when the pace slows.

NINE of WANDS

◆

CONQUEST, TENACITY, RESILIENCE

The Nine of Wands might come at a time when you're feeling worn out and weary, having endured a period of struggle and adversity. You're tired, and for a good reason, but make no mistake: you're resilient and tenacious, and you will continue to fight if you have to.

The woman stands with bandaged head, holding a wand in her hand and reflecting the energy and courage that have carried her this far. Despite the challenges you may have faced, this card reminds you of your capacity to overcome. While you may be tempted to lay down your guard, you are urged to draw on your inner strength and keep pushing forward. Weariness is a testament to your endurance, so embrace the resolute spirit within you, gather your remaining resources, and know that even when you're fatigued victory can be closer than you think.

REVERSED

DEFEAT, EXHAUSTION, BEING OVERWHELMED

A reversed Nine of Wands signifies a deep sense of being overwhelmed and potential defeat. You might find the battles you've faced have taken a toll on your spirit, and the weariness you feel could overshadow your usual resilience and tenacity.

When reversed this card reflects a more vulnerable state than the upright version. The bandaged head and wand in her hand seem to symbolize a lack of readiness to face further challenges. Even the strongest individuals can experience moments of burnout and uncertainty. Instead of pushing forward relentlessly, this is a time to rest, regather your strength, and give yourself permission to seek support. Defeat is not inevitable; it's simply a sign that you need to find new ways to navigate the adversities. By allowing yourself to recharge, you can rise above weariness and find a renewed sense of determination when you're ready to face the battles once more.

TEN of WANDS

◆

SUCCESS, HARD WORK, HEAVY BURDEN

Wow! You've achieved significant success, and now you have a lot on your plate – or, like the woman in the card, a lot on your back. You've taken on so many responsibilities that you're starting to feel weighed down by the amount of pressure you're under to maintain your success. You don't have to take it all on yourself. It is absolutely reasonable to prioritize tasks and drop the less important ones, or delegate work to colleagues, friends, or family members who have more bandwidth than you do. Don't be a martyr, and don't feel obligated to spread yourself thin to please other people.

The woman in the card struggles under the constant twinkling of the wands on her back, always reminding her of the various obligations and tasks she has taken on. Despite the achievements you've realized, the Ten of Wands reminds you that overextending yourself can lead to burnout. As you navigate this period of heightened responsibilities, don't hesitate to seek assistance. Remember that success is not synonymous with shouldering everything alone.

REVERSED

RELEASE, FREEDOM, COLLABORATION

When the Ten of Wands is reversed the burdens that once weighed heavily upon you are now starting to lighten, allowing you to find relief. The constant strain that characterized the upright position is beginning to subside, granting you a chance to reclaim your energy.

A reversed Ten of Wands signifies a moment of unburdening. The woman releases the wands from her back, symbolizing liberation from the responsibilities that were once overwhelming her. This card prompts you to let go of obligations that no longer serve you and reassess your priorities. While success may have been achieved, this is a time to shed unnecessary tasks and regain a sense of spaciousness in your life. Embrace the freedom that comes with releasing the weight of excessive commitments and prioritize your well-being. By releasing what no longer serves you, you can find renewed energy, clarity, and a sense of ease.

PAGE of WANDS

◆

FIRE, ENERGY, POTENTIAL

The Page of Wands is full of pure fire and energy. She has bold ideas and pursues them with passion, but doesn't quite know the right way to execute them. She's working on it and will get there. For this page the journey is just as or more important as the destination, and the road in front of her lights up with potential. The Page of Wands symbolizes a youthful and enthusiastic spirit that is ready to ignite and explore new ideas. She signifies a person on the cusp of creative breakthroughs and exciting ventures. Her fiery energy drives her curiosity and passion, inspiring her to take risks and embrace opportunities. You are encouraged you to embrace your inner spark and channel it into productive avenues. Her youthful outlook reminds you to approach challenges with an open heart and a willingness to learn.

This card prompts you to harness your creative energy, explore your interests, and unlock your hidden talents. By embodying the qualities of the page you can nurture your potential, pursue your dreams, and embark on a journey of self-discovery. Just as fire transforms and illuminates, your energy and enthusiasm can lead to dynamic growth and fulfilling experiences.

REVERSED

DISTRACTION, HASTE, LACK OF INSPIRATION

When reversed, the Page of Wands's usual energetic and creative nature may be disrupted or misguided. Instead of being focused and inspired, she might lack the motivation to pursue her passions. Her haste and impulsive actions could lead to unproductive outcomes and missed opportunities. You are prompted to assess whether your actions are driven by genuine inspiration or a need to simply keep moving. This card also serves as a reminder to slow down, reflect, and find a sense of purpose.

While curiosity is valuable, a reversed Page of Wands advises against being hasty without proper direction. It's a call to re-evaluate your priorities, regain your focus, and seek meaningful sources of inspiration. By cultivating a sense of purpose, you can overcome distractions and once again embrace the spark of creative potential within.

KNIGHT of WANDS

◆

BRAVERY, ADVENTURE, COURAGE

The Knight of Wands is bold, brave, and adventurous, and confidently charges forward in pursuit of her dreams and goals. With the Wands suit representing fire, as does the little salamander, she's a fiery personality and nothing will stand in her way. Depicting a woman charging ahead on her horse while holding a wand in the air, this card signifies a fearless, spirited individual who is ready to embark on bold journeys and fearlessly faces challenges, pursuing her goals with unwavering determination. Her adventurous spirit drives her to explore new horizons, embrace change, and take risks. You are encouraged to follow her example and approach life with a sense of boldness. Her passion and energy will inspire you to embrace your own courage and step out of your comfort zone.

This card prompts you to take on challenges with confidence and enthusiasm. By embodying the qualities of the knight, you can push beyond boundaries and blaze new trails. With bravery and adventure as your guiding principles, you'll inspire those around you to embrace their own journeys with courage.

REVERSED

HESITATION, PASSIVITY, RECKLESSNESS

Reversed, the typical dynamic energy of the Knight of Wands may be compromised or misguided. Instead of charging forward, she may hesitate, overthink, or rush into situations without proper consideration. Her passivity stems from a lack of confidence or fear of the unknown, leading to missed opportunities. When reversed this card prompts you to examine whether your actions are driven by reckless impulses or a reluctance to take necessary risks.

This card serves as a caution against making impulsive decisions that could lead to unintended consequences. It's a call to pause, reassess your direction, and approach challenges with a more measured and thoughtful perspective. While courage is valuable, the reversed version advises against rushing into situations without proper preparation. By finding a balance between boldness and consideration, you can navigate challenges with greater clarity and avoid unnecessary pitfalls.

QUEEN of WANDS

◆

COURAGE, PASSION, CHARISMA

The Queen of Wands radiates good vibes and confidence. When it comes to getting things done, she seems to have a never-ending flow of energy and ideas that she's eager to share with others. It seems as though everything she touches comes alive, and you walk away from her feeling recharged and energized but also wondering what else she has up her sleeve. She's as mysterious as she is powerful, which is represented by the black cat and lioness. She exudes a magnetic energy that draws people toward her. This card signifies a person who fearlessly pursues her dreams with unwavering determination. Her innate courage enables her to take bold steps toward her goals and inspires those around her. She is driven by her passions, and her charismatic presence commands attention and respect.

This card encourages you to tap into your inner fire, embracing your passions with a sense of purpose and confidence. By embodying the qualities of the Queen of Wands you can fearlessly pursue your dreams, inspire others with your charisma, and lead with a fiery spirit that ignites positive change in your own life and the lives of those around you.

REVERSED

INTROVERSION, QUIET STRENGTH, TRANSPARENCY

When reversed this card suggests a shift from outward expression to inner contemplation. The queen's usual fiery energy may be tempered, emphasizing a more reflective and introspective nature. She possesses a quiet strength that comes from within, rather than seeking attention or validation from others. This card prompts you to embrace transparency and authenticity in your interactions, avoiding the need to put on a facade.

While introverted, a reversed Queen of Wands reminds you that quiet strength can be just as impactful as bold charisma. It's a call to use your insights wisely, and exhibit legitimacy in your actions. By embodying these qualities you can navigate challenges with a sense of grace and authenticity.

KING of WANDS

◆

LEADERSHIP, ENTREPRENEURSHIP, VISION

The King of Wands is a natural-born leader and visionary thinker. She sees the big picture and has a gift for conceptualizing short- and long-term projects and mobilizing the right team around her to bring her ideas to fruition. She represents a confident and charismatic figure who is unafraid to take charge and drive her vision forward, and signifies a person who combines her creative spark with practical action to achieve ambitious goals. Her entrepreneurial spirit fuels her ability to lead with passion and inspire those around her. She fearlessly tackles challenges, leveraging her enthusiasm and determination to overcome obstacles.

This card encourages you to embrace your own leadership potential, merging innovative thinking with a pragmatic approach. By embodying the qualities of the King of Wands, you can harness your visionary ideas and inspire others to follow your lead. This dynamic blend of creativity, entrepreneurship, and leadership sets the stage for transformative success in your endeavors.

> ### AUTHOR'S NOTE
>
> In the Rider-Waite-Smith tarot this card has salamanders and lions engraved into the king's throne to represent fire, power, and authority (lion: fire sign, king of the jungle, and salamander: strength, tenacity). I decided to make these animals more prominent to interact with her more actively.

REVERSED
BRUTE FORCE, INEFFECTIVENESS, LACK OF ENERGY

When reversed the King of Wands suggests that her usual dynamic leadership and energy may be diminished or misguided. Instead of channeling her enthusiasm effectively, she may rely on forceful tactics that yield little results. Her lack of energy could stem from a disconnect between her passions and actions. Reversed, this card prompts you to assess whether you're expending your energy in the right direction, and serves as a reminder to avoid pushing ahead without a clear plan. While assertiveness can be powerful, a reversed King of Wands advises against using brute force when subtler strategies would suffice. It's a call to reassess your priorities, and approach challenges with a more strategic mindset. By aligning your actions with your true passions, you can overcome ineffectiveness and lead with renewed vitality.

ACE of CUPS

◆

LOVE, EMOTION, SELF-EXPRESSION

The Ace of Cups suggests that your cup runneth over. You're filled with love and emotion, and it seems to be pouring out of you. You don't need a designated time to embrace your loved ones and hold them close to your heart, but this card gives you a bright green light to do so anyway. Don't hold back from expressing your love to those you hold dear.

A woman holds a cup in her hand and water flows into it, symbolizing the abundance of emotions and depth of your feelings. This card embodies the essence of pure and unconditional love, emotional fulfillment, and the capacity for self-expression, and encourages you to open your heart and allow your emotions to flow freely toward yourself and those around you. Let the waters of your compassion and affection create ripples of connection and understanding, fostering deeper bonds and enriching your relationships. Embrace the opportunity to channel your emotions into creative and meaningful self-expression, nourishing your soul and the hearts of others.

REVERSED

REPRESSION, HESITATION, FOCUS ON SELF

A reversed Ace of Cups suggests a temporary period of emotional repression and hesitation. The overflowing cup now seems to be held back, and the waters of emotions might feel stagnant. You may find yourself holding back from expressing your feelings, possibly due to a fear of vulnerability or past emotional wounds. In this position the focus on self becomes more pronounced. The energies that were once directed outward now turn inward, urging you to explore your emotions, desires, and needs. While this may lead to a sense of self-discovery, it can also result in moments of introspection and withdrawal from others. This card prompts you to take the time you need to understand and process your feelings before opening up to others. Be patient with yourself, and avoid forcing emotional expressions. By prioritizing self-care and addressing your inner world, you can navigate through this phase of hesitancy and find a renewed sense of emotional balance and authenticity.

TWO of CUPS

◆

PARTNERSHIP, CONNECTION, MUTUAL UNDERSTANDING

The Two of Cups signifies a meaningful connection between two people, whether it's a friendship, romantic relationship, or business collaboration. Mutual love and respect flow, and the relationship only grows stronger over time. Two women raise their cups to each other, symbolizing the exchange of emotions and understanding, and the blending of energies. This card celebrates the harmony that results from two people coming together to create something greater than themselves, and is a reminder of the beauty of shared experiences, goals, and emotions.

The energy of the Two of Cups encourages you to embrace the connections that resonate deeply with your heart and soul. This card reminds you of the value of mutual support and empathy, and the enriching exchange of emotions. Celebrate the power of harmonious partnerships and the growth that comes from nurturing these connections with love and care.

REVERSED
BREAK-UP, WITHDRAWAL, MISCOMMUNICATION
OR SELF-LOVE, INDEPENDENCE

A reversed Two of Cups points to a disruption in the harmonious connection that was once present. It signifies challenges in relationships, such as break-ups, misunderstandings, or a sense of withdrawal. The cups that were once raised to each other now seem to be moving apart, reflecting a lack of mutual understanding and miscommunication. Alternatively, this card can suggest a shift toward self-love and independence. The focus turns inward, encouraging you to prioritize your well-being and personal growth. While connections might be strained, this period allows you to explore your own needs and desires, fostering a sense of self-sufficiency and empowerment.

In either interpretation the reversed position prompts you to re-evaluate your relationships and emotions. If facing difficulties, consider whether open communication or seeking resolution is possible. If embracing self-love and independence, use this time to rediscover your strengths and establish a sense of individuality. This card highlights the transformative potential of both challenges and self-discovery on your journey toward greater emotional balance and fulfillment.

THREE of CUPS

◆

SISTERHOOD, SOLIDARITY, FRIENDSHIP

The Three of Cups celebrates women who support one another to celebrate each other's successes. It's a card of collaboration, of working together toward a common goal and toasting their achievements. This card is for friends who pick each other up when someone is down, and indicates a time when you're surrounded by people who love you and want nothing but the best for you and them. The card depicts three women raising their cups in unity, symbolizing sisterhood, solidarity, and friendship. It embodies the essence of joyful connections, shared experiences, and a deep sense of camaraderie. There is strength to be gained from surrounding yourself with individuals who uplift your spirit and celebrate your victories.

As you embrace the energy of the Three of Cups, cherish the bonds you've cultivated and the friendships that support your journey. Whether it's celebrating achievements, providing a shoulder to lean on, or simply sharing laughter, this card encourages you to revel in the beauty of true friendship and the transformative power of friends coming together in mutual love and encouragement.

REVERSED

SOLITUDE, INDEPENDENCE, REFLECTION

A reversed Three of Cups signifies a shift toward solitude, often chosen as a means of fostering independence and self-reflection. While the upright imagery depicts joyful togetherness, this card reversed suggests you're embracing a period of stepping back from social gatherings and focusing on your own company. This time of solitude is not necessarily rooted in isolation but rather in a conscious choice to seek moments of introspection and personal growth. The cups that were once raised in celebration are now held individually, symbolizing a deliberate move toward self-sufficiency.

When reversed this card encourages you to find strength and clarity in solitude. Use this time to explore your thoughts, passions, and desires. As you detach from external distractions you will create space for self-discovery and a deep sense of independence. In moments of quiet reflection you can cultivate a strong sense of self and forge a deeper connection with your inner world.

FOUR of CUPS

◆

MEDITATION, TUNNEL VISION, MISSED OPPORTUNITIES

The Four of Cups shows a woman meditating under a tree, lost in her own thoughts. Beside her are three cups: she either doesn't know they are there, or she's deliberately ignoring them. Another woman offers her a fourth cup, arm outstretched, but she doesn't acknowledge it either.

The Four of Cups signals a time when you're missing out on good things such as invitations and opportunities that are being offered to you. This can be for a couple of reasons: you're focusing so much on what you don't have and what's going wrong that you can't appreciate what you do have or what's going right, or you're feeling so overwhelmed by too many opportunities that you've shut things down to focus internally. It depends on where you are in life at that particular moment. This card can indicate either a need to close yourself off to reflect and evaluate, or to look around and take in the goodness that surrounds you.

REVERSED

INTROSPECTION, SELF-EXPLORATION, INTROVERSION

While the traditional Four of Cups often portrays a woman contemplating her emotions, this reversed interpretation suggests a shift toward seeking solace within yourself. In this position the cups that were once being contemplated now appear more readily accessible, which indicates a potential readiness to explore your inner world, thoughts, and emotions. Rather than being consumed by introspection, you may find you're open to engaging with your thoughts in a more balanced manner.

A reversed Four of Cups encourages you to embrace your introverted tendencies and find comfort in your own company. This period of self-examination will allow you to tap into your inner wisdom and connect with your true desires. Use this time to reflect on your emotions and thoughts, cultivating a deeper understanding of yourself. By honoring your need for solitude and introspection you can gain insights that will contribute to your personal growth and well-being.

FIVE of CUPS

◆

DEPRESSION, REGRET, PESSIMISM

The Five of Cups suggests you may be dwelling on the past and past failures. The woman cries over the three spilled cups in front of her and seems completely unaware of the two full cups behind her. This card urges you to recognize your pain and regret but do everything you can to move on from it. The future is full of possibility, but you need to be in a position to see those opportunities for happiness. Grieve what's gone, build yourself back up and move forward.

This card portrays a moment of sorrow and disappointment, as the spilled cups symbolize what has been lost or left behind. However, the presence of the two remaining cups suggests that hope and potential still exist, even in times of despair. The Five of Cups encourages you to acknowledge your emotions but avoid becoming consumed by them.

Open your eyes to the blessings that remain and the potential for healing and growth. By shifting your perspective and focusing on the full cups you can navigate through difficult emotions and begin to rebuild a sense of optimism and renewal.

REVERSED

PEACE, ACCEPTANCE, PROGRESSION

The reversed Five of Cups suggests that you're moving beyond feelings of loss and embracing a sense of inner tranquility: there is a willingness to let go of past disappointments. This card embodies the themes of finding solace in acceptance and recognizing that healing can come from acknowledging what has been lost while embracing what remains. When reversed this card encourages you to seek peace within yourself, letting go of negativity. This card prompts you to release the weight of past burdens and move forward with a sense of lightness and progress.

SIX of CUPS

◆

NOSTALGIA, PLAY, CHILDHOOD INNOCENCE

The Six of Cups serves to remind you of happy childhood memories. Put aside adult stresses and responsibilities and allow some fun in your life. In this card two children share a moment of joyful exchange, symbolizing nostalgia, play, and the innocence of childhood. This card embodies the essence of reconnecting with the simpler, carefree aspects of life and finding joy in the present moment.

As you embrace the energy of the Six of Cups, consider engaging in activities that spark nostalgia or bring a sense of childlike wonder. Revisiting past hobbies, spending time with loved ones who evoke happy memories, or simply enjoying moments of playfulness can rejuvenate your spirit and offer a break from the demands of adulthood. Embrace the lightheartedness of your inner child and create space for the magic of innocence and joy to permeate your experiences.

> ### AUTHOR'S NOTE
>
> The Six of Cups reminds me a little of the Three of Cups in the way it nudges you to pause and enjoy the moment. Stop and smell the roses – or the daisies and violets, in this case – and tap into your childlike sense of wonder.

REVERSED

HOMESICKNESS, REGRET OR
FORGIVENESS FOR PAST REGRETS

A reversed Six of Cups signals a period when homesickness or a sense of longing for the past becomes more pronounced. Memories and disappointments from earlier times may resurface, causing you to reflect on what has been lost. Alternatively, this card suggests the potential for finding forgiveness for past regrets. In the card a child offers a flower to an adult, symbolizing an opportunity to mend old wounds and seek resolution. By acknowledging past regrets, you can take steps toward releasing their burdens.

Embrace the lessons of the past while also cultivating a sense of acceptance and forgiveness. It's time to heal old wounds and work toward finding peace within yourself. Forgiveness can lead to liberation, allowing you to move forward with a lighter heart and renewed sense of emotional well-being.

SEVEN of CUPS

◆

CHOICES, PREFERENCES, DECISIONS

The Seven of Cups represents a time in your life when you have a lot of options in front of you and need to choose wisely. Gather as much information as you can to make informed decisions and take steps that will serve you well, but be careful because sometimes what seems like a good idea can be a bad one. Think critically and gather all your data to make the best decision for yourself. Don't fall for false illusions or promises. A woman contemplates various cups, each containing a different possibility. This card is a reminder that while opportunities may be abundant, not all of them are equally beneficial or sustainable.

As you embrace the energy of the card, use discernment and careful consideration when making choices. Reflect on your priorities, values, and long-term goals to ensure that the path you choose aligns with your authentic self. By focusing on clarity and avoiding distractions, you can sift through the array of options and move forward with confidence, knowing that you've made choices that will contribute positively to your journey.

REVERSED

CONFUSION, DISTRACTION, AMBIVALENCE

When reversed the once overwhelming array of choices and possibilities in the Seven of Cups may now appear less enticing or more bewildering. When reversed it suggests that confusion or uncertainty could cloud your judgment, making it challenging to make clear decisions. Distractions and conflicting desires may pull your attention in different directions, leading to a sense of ambivalence.

Take a step back and evaluate the options before you. Prioritize clarity and focus, and let go of unrealistic or unfounded fantasies. By addressing the sources of confusion and minimizing distractions, you can regain a sense of direction and purpose. Making deliberate choices that align with your values and goals will guide you through the fog of uncertainty, allowing you to navigate your path with greater intention and determination.

EIGHT of CUPS

◆

TRANSITION, FREEDOM, RELEASE

The Eight of Cups represents actively leaving behind a situation of pain, difficulty, or sadness. The woman leaves her collection of cups to set out on a brand new journey, free and unencumbered. The cups are arranged in a way that looks like one is missing, indicating feelings of disappointment and emptiness, and a lack of fulfillment. She distances herself from the forces that drag her down and moves toward a brighter future. The woman's departure from the cups symbolizes a willingness to let go of what no longer serves her, embracing the unknown with open arms. Recognize when it's time to move on from situations that hinder your growth, because by releasing emotional attachments to the past you create space for new opportunities. Seeking personal freedom and allowing yourself to move forward can lead to a greater sense of fulfillment and alignment with your true path.

REVERSED

INACTION, AVOIDANCE, FEAR OF CHANGE

When this card is reversed, the woman may be hesitant to leave behind a situation that brings discomfort or unease, even if it's not fulfilling. It suggests a resistance to taking the necessary steps for growth and transformation. Fear of the unknown and a reluctance to confront change can lead to a sense of stagnation and missed opportunities. The cups that were left behind in the upright position now remain untouched, reflecting a hesitation to address emotions or circumstances that require attention.

Reflect on whether your current inaction is preventing you from embracing positive change. By addressing your fears you can gradually shift your perspective and move toward a more empowered stance. While stepping into the unknown can be intimidating, it also holds the potential for personal growth and liberation.

AUTHOR'S NOTE

My mom passed away four days before I created this card. As we moved through our grief and tried to reconcile the fact that she was gone, we took comfort in knowing that, like the Eight of Cups, Mom was able to leave behind her pain, fear, and disappointment to finally receive the rest and peace she deserved.

NINE of CUPS

◆

GRATITUDE, SATISFACTION, ACCOMPLISHMENT

You've worked hard to build the life you have, and now is a great time to sit back and take it all in. Really enjoy it, appreciating everything you have and the beauty, love, and support that's all around you. The woman is sitting on a stone wall and is comfortable and content for now, but this will likely change. Life is constantly changing and evolving for better or worse, so all the more reason to take in this moment and appreciate what's happy and fulfilling in your life.

The woman's relaxed posture reflects a sense of contentment, and the arranged cups symbolize the abundant blessings you've gathered through your efforts. Savor the present moment and recognize the achievements and joys that surround you. While life's circumstances may shift, embracing a grateful perspective can bring lasting fulfillment and a deeper connection to the richness of your experiences.

REVERSED

DISSATISFACTION, DISAPPOINTMENT, DISCOURAGEMENT

When reversed the sense of contentment and fulfillment depicted in the upright Nine of Wands may be elusive or tarnished. When turned upside down the woman seems to fall away from the wall she was sitting on, and the cups that were once filled with abundance now appear empty or overturned, reflecting a sense of unfulfilled desires and unmet expectations. The reversed card suggests that despite your efforts, you may be grappling with a lack of satisfaction and a sense of disappointment.

Seek ways to address the root causes of your discontentment. Reflect on whether your expectations are aligned with reality and whether you're setting yourself up for disappointment by placing too much emphasis on external achievements. While life's path can lead to moments of frustration, a reversed Nine of Cups reminds you that shifting your perspective and recalibrating your goals can help you navigate through challenges and find renewed sources of contentment and happiness.

TEN of CUPS

◆

FAMILY, LOVE, FULFILLMENT

The Ten of Cups signifies meaningful relationships and a sense of having worked hard to achieve the life you have. Take a moment to look around and be thankful. The cups arranged in an arc above the family (families?) symbolize blessings and deep emotional connections. The figures beneath the arc of cups reflect a united and harmonious family unit, surrounded by an atmosphere of joy and contentment. This card invites you to celebrate the bonds you share with your loved ones, cherishing the emotional richness and support these connections bring to your life.

As you bask in the warmth of togetherness and love, remember that family can extend beyond blood ties, encompassing chosen relationships that offer you a sense of belonging and acceptance. Embrace the harmony and fulfillment these connections provide, recognizing them as valuable sources of support, happiness, and shared experiences on your journey.

REVERSED
DISHARMONY, CONFLICT, ISOLATION

A reversed Ten of Cups gently addresses themes of disharmony, conflict, and isolation, albeit accompanied by a sense of hope and potential for positive change. While the picture of perfect harmony may seem momentarily disrupted, there's an opportunity for growth and transformation in these challenges. In this position the cups that were once united may now hold the potential for resolution and understanding. Conflict and disharmony can be seen as opportunities for growth and learning, ultimately leading to stronger connections. It's through facing and addressing conflicts that we often gain deeper insights into ourselves and others.

Approach conflicts with an open heart and willingness to listen and understand. While isolation may feel present, remember that bridges can be rebuilt through communication and empathy. By taking steps to address conflicts and work toward harmony, you can transform the situation into one that fosters a renewed sense of togetherness and ultimately leads to greater understanding and connection.

PAGE of CUPS

♦

IDEALISM, CURIOSITY, BRAVERY

The Page of Cups opens her heart and mind to all possibilities. She wholeheartedly believes anything is possible and doesn't let anyone underestimate her abilities or dictate what she's capable of. She's curious, brave, and on the lookout for opportunities and surprises, represented by the fish popping out of the water. She raises her cup high and proud, optimistic that it'll be filled with whatever she truly needs at that moment. She approaches life with a sense of wonder, and a heart full of dreams. This card signifies a youthful spirit unafraid to explore new emotions and experiences. Her idealism drives her to seek beauty and connection in the world around her. Embrace your curiosity and open-mindedness, approaching challenges with a fresh perspective. The page's bravery stems from her willingness to engage with her emotions and navigate vulnerability.

Fearlessly pursue your passions and nurture your creative spirit. When you embrace your idealistic nature and dare to explore the unknown you can inspire others to welcome their dreams and cultivate lives rich with meaning and wonder. Just as she offers her cup of emotions to the world, you can offer your unique insights and bravery to create a positive impact.

REVERSED
CREATIVE BLOCK, VULNERABILITY, IMMATURITY

This reversal suggests that the usual creative flow of the Page of Cups may be obstructed, causing frustration and a sense of stagnation. Her vulnerability might become more pronounced, making her quite sensitive to emotional fluctuations. Her immaturity could manifest as a lack of emotional understanding or impulsivity in expressing feelings. When reversed this card prompts you to address deep-seated creative barriers and approach vulnerability with caution and self-awareness.

Navigate creative challenges with patience and self-compassion. The card encourages you to seek guidance to overcome creative blocks and responsibly navigate heightened emotions. By addressing emotional immaturity and practicing self-care, you can find ways to manage vulnerability, unleash your creative potential, and develop a more mature and profound connection with your artistic pursuits.

KNIGHT of CUPS

◆

EMPATHY, CHARM, HUMANITY

The Knight of Cups wears her heart on her sleeve and is in touch with her emotions. She has a deep sense of empathy that helps her genuinely, compassionately relate to others. People are attracted to her mysterious charm and ability to find beauty in all things. Depicting a woman on a horse holding a cup out into the darkness, she symbolizes an individual who approaches life with a deep understanding of others' emotions and a genuine desire to connect, even in the darkest of times. Her charm is not merely superficial; it stems from a heartfelt empathy that resonates with people. Tap into your emotional intelligence and use your charm to foster authentic connections.

Embrace your ability to relate to others and use your charm to spread kindness. By embodying the qualities of the Knight of Cups you can navigate challenges with empathy, inspire through your actions, and foster a more compassionate and harmonious environment. Just as she rides forth with her cup of emotional connection, you can lead with your heart and make a meaningful difference in the lives of those around you.

REVERSED

JEALOUSY, MOODINESS, PREOCCUPATION

A reversed Knight of Cups embodies themes of disrupted empathy, misdirected charm, and challenges in connecting with humanity. The knight's usual ability to emotionally connect with others might be compromised and her charm could become superficial, lacking the depth of true empathy and being used to manipulate rather than uplift. Her interactions may not reflect genuine concern for others. Assess whether your interactions are sincere or driven by ulterior motives.

Reconnect with authentic empathy and genuine humanity in your interactions. When reversed this card encourages you to use your charm in a way that truly benefits others and fosters meaningful connections. By embodying the qualities of the reversed Knight of Cups with sincere intentions, you can navigate challenges with integrity and create a more harmonious and genuine environment around you.

QUEEN of CUPS

◆

COMPASSION, EMPATHY, INNER CALM

The Queen of Cups is intuitive, creative, and nurturing. She's sensitive, compassionate, and empathetic but doesn't take on any negative energy that may surround her. She dips her toe in the water, which in the tarot represents emotions, feelings, and the subconscious, but doesn't submerge herself in it. She represents a deeply nurturing and intuitive figure who is in touch with her emotions and the emotions of others. This card signifies a person who embodies a gentle and supportive presence. Her compassion extends to those around her, as she is able to offer solace and understanding without judgment. Tap into your emotional intelligence and connect with your intuition. The queen's inner calm serves as a beacon of tranquility, even amid chaos.

You can create a safe space for emotional expression, foster deep connections, and navigate challenges with a sense of empathy. Just as the queen balances her emotions, intuition, and compassion, you can find harmony within yourself and positively impact those in your life.

> ### AUTHOR'S NOTE
>
> My interpretation of this card emphasizes the ground she stands on, particularly the rocks. She holds one of the rocks in her hand, about to drop it in the water. With this action she interacts with the earth and the sea at once on her own terms.

REVERSED

NEEDINESS, CLINGINESS OR DETACHMENT, HYPERSENSITIVITY

The Queen of Cups reversed suggests that her typical emotional depth may become magnified to an extent where she becomes overly reliant on others for validation and security. Her hypersensitivity could lead to being emotionally overwhelmed and difficulty in maintaining healthy boundaries. When reversed this card serves as a caution against losing yourself in emotional demands and excessively seeking reassurance.

Assess whether your emotional responses are stifling your personal growth. It's crucial to recognize the importance of self-sufficiency and setting boundaries. When reversed this card calls for mindful consideration of your emotional needs and finding ways to address them independently. By addressing tendencies toward neediness and cultivating inner strength, you can navigate your emotions with greater resilience and authenticity.

KING of CUPS

◆

MODERATION, SERENITY, BALANCE

The King of Cups represents balanced emotions and temperament, and a healthy balance between caution and fearlessness. She reaches out, unafraid, into the unknown. Her fish necklace indicates creativity, which thrives in an environment of calm and balance. She is a compassionate and composed individual who navigates emotions with wisdom and equilibrium. This card signifies a person who maintains emotional harmony and understands the importance of measured responses.

This card encourages you to cultivate a similar sense of balance between your feelings and actions. The king's serene presence fosters a safe space for others to express their emotions without judgment. Embrace a calm and measured approach to your emotional life because, by embodying the qualities of the King of Cups, you can navigate situations with grace, offering support and understanding to others while maintaining your emotional equilibrium. Just as she skillfully manages the ebb and flow of emotions, you can find tranquility in the delicate dance of moderation and balance.

REVERSED

OVERREACTION, ANXIETY OR SELF-COMPASSION

When overcome by overreaction and anxiety, the King of Cups loses the serene balance depicted in her upright form. She struggles to keep her emotions in check, and her fish necklace becomes a heavy burden. This card reminds you to practice self-compassion, as she navigates choppy emotional waters. Amid the storm, find equilibrium.

ABOUT
THE AUTHOR

Heidi Phelps is an American writer and artist from Washington, DC. She created the *Black Violet Taro*t as she became a mother and while losing her own mother to cancer. Illustrated entirely in black and white, this tarot deck reflects that idea of bittersweet dualities, of shining a light in times of darkness. Heidi's diverse list of artistic influences includes Edward Gorey, Victorian-era mourning costumes and memento mori, vintage early to mid-century sewing patterns, Grimm's fairy tales, Salvador Dali's Alice in Wonderland sketches, Henri de Toulouse-Lautrec, Frida Kahlo, and Marjane Satrapi. When she's not sketching – and even when she is – Heidi spends time with her husband Erdem, her daughter Leyla, and her two cats Eddie and Daisy.

blackvioletdc | www.heidiphelps.art